W9-COF-872

SOUL

TRAVELER

A Guide to Out-of-Body Experiences and the Wonders Beyond

SOUL TRAVELER
A Guide to Out-of-Body Experiences and the Wonders Beyond
By Albert Taylor

Published by:
Verity Press Publishing
P. O. Box 31
Covina, CA 91723

Library of Congress Catalog Number: 95-94746

ISBN: 0-9647534-6-4

Printed in the United States of America

1 2 3 4 5 6 7 8 9 0

DISCLAIMER

This publication is designed to give the experience of one man who desires to provide information to those who may experience the same type of paralysis as he has, in order to help to alleviate their fears and perhaps show how they too can cross the threshhold to achieve an out-of-body experience. This publication is in no way responsible for harm to others and stresses that attempting an out-of-body experience is at the reader's own risk.

Original front cover art by Albert Taylor. Page and cover design by One-on-One Book Production, California

To my son

DEVON

*Without your love I would not have had the courage to
venture as far as I did.
You are my dream child, and my shining star.
All my love forever, Dad.*

MY SPECIAL THANKS TO:

Shirley MacLaine

Beatrice Scott

Jack Houck

Pat Lewis

Kim Craven

Dr. Carole Carbone

Susan Walker

IANDS

Luz Virgen

Daryll Ford

Constance Ray

Nancy Henderson

The Learning Light Foundation

Catherine Coleman

and Otto-Matic

Table of Contents

FOREWORD

Albert Taylor, engineer/scientist and artist began his childhood marked by the mysterious. He would often experience a type of paralysis during the night and the early morning hours. Told by his grandmother that "The witches are riding you," young Albert sought a more definitive explanation. His accompanying search for the truth is one of courage and love. *SOUL TRAVELER* is a story that belongs to each of us. With Albert Taylor, we experience the mysterious, rejoice in the enlightenment and are awed at the infinite capabilities of the human mind and soul.

Albert Einstein once said: "The most beautiful thing we can experience is the mysterious, it is the source of all true art and science." Albert Taylor truly lived that statement.

Dr. Carole Carbone

INTRODUCTION

> *Many wondrous gifts have been bestowed upon all of us in this life, but each shall be revealed in its own time and place. If you know this to be true, then you too shall fly.*
>
> **—Soul Traveler**

Is there life beyond death's door? Does the human soul really exist? Are angels and ghosts real? Are these spiritual beings helping to shape mankind's destiny?

I believe I have found some answers to these questions. In truth, the answers have literally found me. Within these pages I have attempted to describe my soul travels, also known as Out-of-Body Experiences or OBEs.

First, I must say that I am not what you would call a religious person. Although I was baptized Catholic and served as an altar boy, I have not attended church regularly in years. I would also say that I have not had a life filled with psychic occurrences. However, there are two out of the ordinary events I find difficult to ignore. One of these is a type of "paralysis" I would experience during the night and early morning. The other involves my father which will be explained later in these writings.

The primary focus to begin with will be an explanation of the paralysis. "The witches are riding you!" is what my grandmother would say whenever someone complained about the paralysis. This so-called paralysis, I found out later, was my own personal doorway to what may be the "ultimate truth."

All my life, as far back as I can remember, I have had a peculiar thing happen to me that I simply dreaded. All too often I woke up fully aware of my surroundings; I could hear and see, but I was totally incapable of moving. I was paralyzed! I call this the "paralysis state." My only understanding of the paralysis at that time was that it happened to my mother, my cousin Robert and myself; and we *all* hated it!

A few years later when I was told that Robert had died, I learned that he was in the paralysis state when he passed on. Catherine, Robert's wife, said her husband was moaning, which was their signal for her to shake/wake him up. Normally, this was enough to rouse him, but Robert soon stopped moaning and slipped away.

This unwelcome news about Robert only added to the difficulty I already had for this. . .this. . .this defect. I not only hated the paralysis, I started to fear it. I now thought I was on the verge of death when I was in the paralysis. For

Introduction

years I "suffered" with this "affliction." I found out early that during the paralysis, I was only capable of moaning aloud like Robert; nothing more. I will label this "abort sequence." My wife, Kathy, became so accustomed to this that she would nudge me with her elbow to wake me. I would then be capable of moving my body again.

So, that was the situation. I woke up in the paralysis, moaned slightly (abort sequence), and Kathy elbowed me. I hated it! I didn't have a clue as to how close I was to achieving an OBE. OBE is one term that is currently used, astral projection is another, but I prefer to call it "soul travel." I use this term for a variety of reasons. One of them is because of a group known as the Eckankar Society, but more on that later.

Another peculiar thing that happened during sleep is what I used to call "waking up in my dreams." Although sound asleep, I became cognizant that I was dreaming, or at least aware of what I thought was a dream. Scientific and metaphysical circles refer to this as "lucid dreaming."

After waking up in my dream, I changed the dream! Sometimes I would fly. Other times, I explored my sur-roundings. It wasn't always easy to keep my thoughts focused, but when I did it was always exciting. These occurrences, the paralysis state, waking up in my dreams, and flying remained non-connected for most of my childhood and adult life.

One evening I rented the movie "Out On A Limb," starring Shirley MacLaine. This film had a profound impact on me; one that I could not understand at that time. At the end of the film, Shirley MacLaine had an OBE resulting from a series of spiritual events. I was so affected by this movie that I wrote Shirley MacLaine a letter (that I never mailed). It read:

Dear Shirley MacLaine,

I am not in the habit of writing or contacting celebrities as a fan or otherwise. But writing to you is something I feel compelled to do.

Recently my wife and I viewed your film on video, "Out on a Limb," after which we both were deeply affected; I more than her. It has been two weeks since then, and I still feel undeniably affected by this film.

Presently, I am an engineer on NASA's Space Station Freedom program, and have worked in aerospace for the last two decades on various government classified and non-classified programs. I consider myself lucky enough to have been exposed to projects that most Americans won't hear about for years to come, if ever.

All my life I have been and continue to be interested in astronomy, space travel, UFOs, and psychic phenomena. I don't want you to get the impression that my only interest is in space related areas. I just wanted to give you an idea of my background, in hopes of adding some credibility to this letter.

Well, to make a long story short, I am seeking knowledge about life-past, present, and future. I'd like to know more about astral projection. I'd like to know more about the Force that is in and around us. I would like to discover the connection between out of body experiences and this Force.

In conclusion, I wanted to tell you that I applaud your courage in coming forth with your discoveries. In

Introduction

doing so, you have subjected yourself to ridicule among your peers and the media. It seems to me that you have put everything on the line for what may be the ultimate truth. So if you can find time in your busy schedule, I would appreciate suggestions from you on a direction or path to follow.

Sincerely,
Albert Taylor Jr.

P.S. Thanks for sharing what you have, by way of the video "Out On A Limb."

I became semi-obsessed with the thought of having an OBE. I shared my interest with a close friend who suggested I take a metaphysical course taught by Doctor H. at the local college. My wife and I signed up for Part I of a series of lectures/workshops that Doctor H. developed and taught. Having had a near death experience and witnessing a host of psychic occurrences, Doctor H. was driven to teach classes which focused on spiritual awareness and enlightenment.

During the course Doctor H. asked the class a question that would profoundly change my life. She asked if anyone ever felt *paralyzed* at night after lying down to sleep.

Oh my God! I thought the paralysis was mine alone! Well, mine, my mother's, and my deceased cousin Robert's.

Doctor H. began to describe how this paralysis was related to OBEs. I immediately doubted her because I *knew* that I had not had an OBE.

Doctor H. then said, "You can't tell me what you don't know!" She also described how flying dreams may very well be OBEs. I thought, "no way! I fly all the time!" I left the class puzzled and a little more excited. Could this be true? Are my flying dreams OBEs?

At that point, I needed to investigate. I went out and bought every book on OBEs and astral projection I could find. Robert Monroe's *Journeys Out of the Body,* and Dr. Keith Harary and Pamela Weintraub's *Out of Body Experiences,* were a couple out of many I read. Monroe's books fascinated and scared me.

Why did there have to be disembodied entities in his writing? Doesn't he know that I am afraid of ghosts, even though I have no justifiable reason?

His book triggered memories. There was the time I was about four years old, when during the paralysis, a figure sat at the end of my bed and whispered my name.

"Al l l b e r r r t!"

I remember another time at the age of seven, I lay at the foot of my parent's bed watching the Louis Lomax Show. Mr. Lomax was interviewing a man who claimed to have captured the ghostly images of monks, praying in a three or four century old English cathedral. The blurry soft white figures kneeling among the cathedral pews scared me so much I refused to go to bed. Finally my mother convinced me to go to bed clutching a set of Catholic rosary beads close to my chest, and reciting the "Hail Mary" prayer over and over again. I have no idea

Introduction

why I have such a strong fear of ghosts, entities, or spirits. After all, it's not as if there are such things,right?

I soon learned that fear would be the bars in a prison of my own creation. It is important to realize that fear is a very effective self-created road block. I cannot stress this **_enough._**

Soul Traveler

1

AIRBORNE

> *"I want to fly more than anything else in the world!"*
> **—Richard Bach,**
> **Jonathan Livingston Seagull**

In February 1993, I decided to visit my regular physician, in hopes of unraveling some of the mystique surrounding the paralysis. As I sat there in the modest examination room, I rehearsed how I was going to phrase my questions regarding the paralysis.

"Uh...Doctor, have you ever had a patient who couldn't get up while sleeping?" (The answer to this would likely be "Yes, all of them!")

"Doctor, I lose control of my body at night." (Sounds like demonic possession.)

"Hey Doc, I have concerns about being paralyzed." (This sounds like paranoia.)

"Good afternoon Doctor! I've been meaning to tell you about my paralysis." (A bit too casual.)

"Doctor I have a..." (she walked into the room).

"Hello Mr. Taylor," she said. "How are you?"

She began to examine me. During the exam she asked so many questions, I hardly got a word in edgewise. Finally she paused.

"Doctor," I said. "Have you ever awakened in the middle of the night feeling paralyzed?"

She looked at me and smiled, "Don't worry about it, that happens to me sometimes. You'll be alright!"

"But I'm not..."

"You're in good health Mr. Taylor. See you in three months." She turned and walked out. It was clear this meant that I was on my own, for now.

14 March 93, 10:00 P.M. (Fearful)

I went to bed a little afraid. I drifted off to sleep not really knowing what I should do to achieve an OBE. I really wasn't sure what to do if anything, except sleep.

☾ OBE BEGINS

I thought something grabbed my right arm. The next thing I knew I was lying in the bed in the paralysis. I fought my way out of the paralysis, partially sat up in the bed, and looked at the clock. It was 3:00 A.M., Sunday morning.

❧   ❧   ❧

15 March 93, 9:30 P.M. (Moderately tired)

I settled into bed, relaxed my body, and surrounded myself with white light (what I now refer to as training wheels). A number of the tools and techniques I used in the beginning are like training wheels on a child's bike. After a certain amount of practice I no longer needed them. I soon drifted off into a light sleep.

☾ OBE BEGINS

The next thing I knew I was flying better and faster than I've ever flown. I thought to myself, "Wow, I did it!" I thought about visiting Doctor H. as she had suggested.

I changed directions and zipped off. On the way there, I experimented with speed and altitude. I thought about speeding up, and I did. I thought about flying higher, and I did. Down below I saw houses, trees, and neighborhood streets melted together into one continuous blur. Never had I traveled so fast. No car, train, or plane could match the speed I was traveling. I slowed my velocity and became aware that I was being drawn down toward the roof of a house that was rapidly getting larger and closer.

I entered the room through the wall and floated up to the foot of a bed. I thought that I was in a hospital room because a bright white figure, whom I thought to be a nurse, was standing next to the person in the bed.

As I approached the foot of the bed, the white figure backed away. Doctor H. was lying in the bed and did not appear to be awake. Suddenly without moving, mentally I heard her say, "Congratulations Al; you did it."

"I know!" I replied.

We were communicating but not with just words. Not only could I hear her voice, I felt the mood in which she said it. I also noticed that she and her husband did not sleep in the same bed. I thought this would be something worth verifying when I saw her physically, primarily because I still wasn't convinced that I was really here. I could be dreaming! I experienced a quick visual shift, some rapid movement, and was back in bed, connected. I sat up on my elbows and thought, "Wow, that was great!" I turned over on my side and fell asleep.

★ RETROSPECT

How could Doctor H. see and hear me? Was I dreaming? I would later learn that the soul can communicate with other souls but not necessarily with the awareness of the "personality self." The "personality self" is the part of us that interfaces with our every day material world. It is this part of the psyche that hates, fears, envies, and judges—some of our best qualities!

Later that week my wife and I attended another OBE class. I could hardly wait to talk to Doctor H. but I held back and decided to approach her at the break. I greeted her and asked, "So Doctor H., did anything happen over the weekend?"

Doctor H. said she remembered seeing me in her dream but could not recall the details of the dream. She also said she remembered me turning away from her like I was leaving. I then began to describe Doctor H.'s bedroom and shared with her that I noticed she and her husband slept in separate beds. Doctor H. looked at me and smiled, "Yes, that is correct!"

I wondered if the entire event was just a weird coincidence? Doctor H. only remembered me in her dream, and I didn't want to read more into it than what she actually said. Although I was hoping that she would have remembered a little more. (I counted this whole "visit" as a maybe.)

❧   ❧   ❧

16 March 93, 10:00 P.M. (Fearful)

I decided not to attempt an OBE. I also had trouble surrounding myself with white light. In time I would cease to use the white light because I believe its use stems from fear. Later, I woke up in the middle of the night vibrating. I crossed my arms, turned over on my left side, and fell asleep.

★ RETROSPECT

The "vibrations" (or "vibes") I felt have happened numerous times, but I always thought they were earth tremors. Living in California I didn't pay much attention to the experiences at first, but later I realized that the "vibes" were more pieces to the puzzle.

22 March 93, 4:00 P.M. (Relaxed)

I tried to fall asleep. I finally dropped off, then woke a short while later with my body vibrating. I looked for signs of an earthquake, of which there were none. Feeling very tired, I soon fell back to sleep.

28 March 93, 9:30 P.M. (Tired and sleepy)

This was the first time I used a relaxation tape. I performed the exercises and drifted off into a light sleep. Shortly thereafter I woke and noticed the tape was half over (about 20 minutes had passed). I took off the head phones and fell asleep.

☾ OBE BEGINS

I was walking on a sidewalk. I stopped suddenly because I was puzzled as to how I got there. I then thought, "Is this a dream?"

In the past, when I've become lucid in my dreams, I perform a simple test to verify my suspicions. I would attempt to fly low over the ground. I focused my thoughts, leaned forward, and I flew slowly over the sidewalk.

I stood up, looked around and thought, "Alright! I did it again!" I continued to check out my surroundings which were illuminated by a strange glow. It wasn't dark nor was it daylight; it was an eerie dusk. The lighting did not appear to have a one directional source. I leaned forward and took off flying over the city. . .or "a city." I had no idea where I was. Soon I flew over a neighborhood...somewhere. Below me I saw what looked like a swimming pool. I decided to experiment. I flew into the water. At first I held my breath because I didn't want to be the first to drown astrally. I decided to take in a breath. I could feel cool water all around me, then the coolness came into me as I inhaled. I thought, "This is incredible!"

I surfaced then dove under again and experienced the same exhilaration. I became aware that two or three figures stood just beyond the edge of the pool, and slightly beyond my vision. I felt as if the figures were observing me like a teacher monitoring a playground. To avoid a possible encounter, I flew out of the water and into the sky. Wherever I was, I could see many roof tops close together.

Suddenly, there was a loud crash. I opened my physical eyes, sat up in bed blurting out, "Jesus!"

Kathy stood at the end of the bed smiling sheepishly. "Sorry!" she said. "I dropped the flashlight."

❂　　❂　　❂

30 March 93, 12:00 A.M. Midnight (Very sleepy)

I attempted an OBE. I lay flat on my back trying to relax and clear my mind. After what felt like an eternity, I began to feel a low level tingle slowly increase to full blown vibration. I was a little surprised because this was the first time I started the vibrations before falling asleep, so I really didn't know what to expect.

At some point during the vibes, I felt several strong surges, then fear set in. I crossed my arms, turned over on my left side, and fell asleep.

April 93, 3:30 A.M. (Woke up, after sleeping)

I woke up and had difficulty going back to sleep, so I decided to attempt the vibes with the help of a relaxation tape. Halfway into it I stopped the tape and turned over. I felt myself begin vibrating. I turned over on my back and tried to increase the vibes. The vibes surged from deep within me like the foreshocks of a California earthquake—with my head being the epicenter.

☾ OBE BEGINS

I thought about floating upward. I felt the top of my head rubbing against the headboard of our bed. The headboard had begun to slide downward!

I could actually feel the surface of the headboard moving away from me, or was I moving away from it? Then suddenly I could see, but my physical eyes were not open!

I noticed an eerie, non-directional lighting radiating inside our bedroom. I also became aware of an intermittent, high volume buzzing sound. I thought to myself, "Is this it?" I decided to get up physically, but I could not move an inch! I was paralyzed! This realization shocked me and caught me completely off guard.

This was the first time that I experienced the paralysis without sleeping first, then waking into it. Without the slightest bit of warning, a humanoid shape appeared on my right about eighteen inches away from me. It startled me. I mentally told it to move away from me. It did not respond! But it did become increasingly transparent.

I panicked! I initiated the abort sequence, hoping that Kathy would wake me up, which she did. The lighting in the room changed as I reconnected with my body.

After waking I told Kathy about the ghostly apparition. She explained to me that I had not moved physically, and my head was approximately nine inches from the headboard when she nudged me. I was about that far away from the headboard before I fell asleep. Remarkable!

★ RETROSPECT

I wasn't exactly afraid of the figure near me. I think that the buzzing sound, the lighting, floating, the paralysis, and finally the figure, all overwhelmed me. Kathy described my head as being physically nine inches away from the headboard, yet I could actually feel the uneven button tucking of the vinyl surface. Did I astral project out of the top of my head?

I've read in various books that it is very common to astral project through the top of the head. I find it amusing that a couple of books would use the word "common." To me none of this is common!

24 April 93, 9:30 P.M. (Tired)

I decided to use the relaxation tape again. While laying there feeling very relaxed, a brilliant light flashed across my eyelids. It was blue and was accompanied by a zipping or buzzing sound. I briefly pondered on the significance of this, then fell asleep.

1 May 93 (Woke up after sleeping)

I woke up in the paralysis feeling a little frightened but talked myself out of it.

☾ OBE BEGINS

I tried a different way to leave this time. I remembered reading in Robert Monroe's book, *Journeys Out of the Body,* that an alternate way to get out of the body was to "roll out." I thought of rolling over, and I did. I then realized I was looking down at my wife's face. I was floating about 12 inches or so directly above her. I was also aware of a presence in the room, but it seemed content to stay near the television.

I tried to stand up feeling for the blanket with my *astral feet*. I noticed the blankets weren't solid; my foot pushed through with very little effort. Next I felt the vinyl surface of the waterbed mattress, and with the slightest pressure I was able to push through to the heated water underneath. The plywood support panel underneath the mattress resisted at first, then gave way to my probing appendage.

I pushed through the plywood to the carpet below. I couldn't believe it! I stood there in the middle of the bed moving my astral feet around in the carpet! Incredible! I looked around the room when the thought of venturing further crossed my mind, and with that thought, I must have drifted into a uncontrollable dream state.

★ RETROSPECT

The aforementioned is a strange way to end an OBE. Normally I remember returning, but not this time. Could it be that my jaunts are being guided by some unseen force, which is allowing me to experience OBEs in small doses at a time?

I wonder if the majority of people have OBEs but lose consciousness or drift into the "normal" dream state, as I must have. An important key to this question might be to remain consciously aware, but this appears to be easier said than done.

Soul Traveler

2

BUZZING BEES

Doctor H. has been a tremendous resource of information, and shared many techniques as well. She told me she taught another class which specifically focused on OBEs and suggested I attend. She also invited me to join her at an International Association of Near Death Studies (IANDS) group meeting held in Santa Fe Springs, California. I was looking forward to attending both.

The class turned out to be a great help. I was not only exposed to historically documented cases but met individuals eager to understand experiences similar to mine. Most of the students were hoping to have their first OBE.

After the third and final out of body class, I expressed to Doctor H. my dislike of the paralysis and asked if she had any pointers on controlling or tolerating it.

"When you feel paralyzed, just think of moving your little finger; you'll reconnect," she said. It turned out to be as simple as that. With this added bit of information, I could reconnect with my body with very little effort.

No more panic, and no more fighting my way out of it. Where had this woman been all my life? Because of her I stopped dreading the paralysis and actually looked forward to it.

In July 1993, I attended my first IANDS group meeting. I found the first hand accounts of it's members' near death experiences (NDEs) fascinating. One woman had three NDEs as the result of a liver disease. Another woman had a car accident which forced her and her son (a passenger) both to have simultaneous NDEs.

Feeling uneasy about sharing my OBEs, I became a good listener. After all, these people had experienced death. I was just performing reconnaissance missions. The members would repeatedly refer to the woman who had experienced three NDEs whenever the subject of OBEs came up.

I was told as a result of the three NDEs, Rosanna continues to have conscious, controlled OBEs. And far more often than anyone else they knew. I had to meet her! To make a long story short, Rosanna and I met and became good friends. She shared with me her NDEs as well as her OBEs. I felt very comfortable with her and shared some of my jaunts. We exchanged books, relaxation tapes, and conversation.

26 September 93, 1:30 A.M. (A little sleepy)

Nothing has happened in four months. I got up at 1:30 A.M. because I couldn't sleep. I stayed up until 4:30 A.M. Shortly after going back to bed I started my own "pre-flight routine" that I've developed since my experiences began.

☾ OBE BEGINS

I felt my legs floating upward. I marveled at this! I moved my legs downward and right through the mattress. I kept doing this for a minute or so. Up and down, up and down. My *astral* legs didn't feel like my physical legs; they felt rubbery or elastic. I noticed that I could extend them or wrap them around each other forming an astral pretzel. I could also change their size and shape at will.

Then something happened that would permanently alter my OBEs. The softest, kindest female voice that I have ever heard spoke into my ear.

"Al,...?"

I panicked, again! Someone, or something, was gently holding my arms. The grip was more protective than restraining.

I initiated the abort sequence. Kathy was right on time. I reconnected and sat up.

★ RETROSPECT

Well, not only had I seen, felt, and heard an apparition; but it decided to communicate. I guess if it wasn't aware of my fear of spirits before, it is now!

I told a friend at work whom I trust about the strange occurrences. She said I should visit the Eckankar Society. Eckan who? Never heard of it! Given the fact I am a native of Southern California, I wondered why I had never heard of this "Eckankar Society." Finding the Eck society wasn't difficult. The main office is located in Anaheim, California.

On September 27, 1993, I drove to Anaheim. I walked into the front door interrupting a group of people sitting in a circle in the middle of the room. A middle aged woman smiled at me, motioning for me to take a seat, which I did as quickly as possible. They all closed their eyes and began to sing the strangest song. I joined in trying not to stand out.

After they completed what I now know to be the "Hu," they began to discuss dreams and how they were influenced by spiritual masters. After a short while I raised my hand, hoping they would allow me to speak.

"Yes?" The woman asked with curiosity.

I answered. "Uh, I've never been here before, and I was wondering what this was all about."

"You fit in so well we all thought you were an Eckist."

"He even Hu'd with us!" Another person remarked.

I was then greeted as if I were a long, lost relative. I must admit that I have never before been greeted by strangers who openly and genuinely expressed such love for me. I told them about my experiences and that I was searching for understanding. One woman left and soon returned with a chart that depicted the various levels of consciousness.

She pointed to the etheric level. The sound associated with that level is "buzzing bees!" These people had a chart that listed the sound that I heard. Wasn't this a validation? They then began to explain to me the meaning of Eckankar.

I was told that Eckankar means co-worker with God. They believe that is the ultimate destiny of the soul and that this purpose can only be achieved through the lessons learned from numerous reincarnational lives. One of the men directed me to their in-house library, informing me that I was welcome to take home any of their books or cassette tapes as long as I returned them.

Over the next few months, I was to learn many things from the Eckist. The Eckankar Society practices a number of spiritual exercises to help a person accomplish a variety of things, including "soul travel."

An interesting point is that the Eckist would tell me that they do not consider themselves to have a soul. "We are soul," they would profess with conviction. They would also refer to the energy we accept as life as the "Eck."

After I purchased a book from the Eckist's library I left.

The book was about a man who learned to soul travel. The book suggested several spiritual exercises. One described going to bed early and setting an alarm to wake up at 1:30 AM. Get out of bed, stay up for a couple of hours, and do not eat or drink anything except water. Go back to bed.

This sounded like what I experienced September 26, 1993. Was it? Or was it just a coincidence?

The author continued. Chant the "Hu" (pronounced like the name Hugh). The Hu was described as a love song to God. The Hu is chanted by taking a deep breath and slowly letting it out through parted lips, singing one long continuous Hu.

A second book listed over one hundred different spiritual exercises to aid a person in psychic achievements, clairvoyance, spiritual healing, past life regression, and of course soul travel.

I've tried the interrupted sleep technique (or IST) with phenomenal success; eight OBEs out of ten attempts! One night I woke up in the paralysis, relaxed, and let go of the physical. I felt as if I was being bounced, then shaken up and down on the bed. I mentally projected, "Stop it!" I did so just in case someone or something was responsible.

Later that year I attended the Eckankar World Seminar at the Los Angeles Convention Center. It was amazing that an organized society of this magnitude would be virtually unknown, at least in my limited circle. To my mystification, here were over 2,000 people from all over the world: Spain, England, Africa, Germany; and all of them believed in the soul leaving the body.

My primary reason for attending the seminar was to meet someone experiencing psychic occurrences similar to mine. To my disappointment most of the people were hoping to achieve soul travel or had their focus in other areas, such as healing and predicting the future or exploring past lives.

"We were hoping to get where *you* are!" A few of them said.

"Where *I* am?" I thought to myself. "And where exactly is that?" I felt fortunate and disappointed at the same time.

I was looking for a spiritual master to take me under his wing and teach me the forgotten knowledge of the "ancient ones." Although I desperately tried, I was unable to make this a reality. All in all, I spent most of the day with people who were just kind, loving, and considerate. Everyone there communicated a sense of inner peace.

During a ten day experiment between October 7 and October 17, 1993, I had three OBEs in one night. Two of the OBEs began unlike any of the previous ones.

15 October 93 (IST)

I performed an abbreviated pre-flight routine.

☾ OBE BEGINS

I lay there until I became aware of a small scene forming between my eyes. As I stared at the picture, it grew larger and larger until I was standing in it. I was near what looked like a neighborhood street corner.

Wow, that was different! I looked around and realized again that I had no idea where I was. I felt brave and asked to see my guide, pointing to a spot right in front of me...well, about 10 feet in front of me. That was close enough for a first time meeting, right?

I repeated my request but he/she/it was a "no-show." I thought of my body and wondered how easy it would be to return. Before I could complete the thought, there was a quick visual shift and rapid movement; and I was slammed back into my body! In spite of the rough landing, I tried not to move.

I lay still, and soon there was another picture in what I now know is my "third eye." I experienced the same sequence of events; the picture grew larger and larger until I stood in it.

This time I leaned forward and flew up into the sky. I felt like Jonathan Livingston Seagull as I soared around appreciating an incredible view of green hillsides dotted with an occasional house or apartment building. Feeling a strange urge to return, I thought of my body, experienced a visual blur, entered, and reconnected.

★ RETROSPECT

Reconnecting with my body has become quite natural. I no longer feel helpless. I merely think of moving my little finger, and presto! This has decreased the time I spend in the paralysis significantly. However, I still find discomfort in the sensations that accompany the paralysis state. The difficulty in breathing and the fading physical awareness almost feels as if I am dying. Don't misunderstand me, it is not painful in anyway, just very discomforting. The paralysis state, I believe, is like experiencing death in a small dose; sort of a mini-death. In a way, it is the halting of one existence and the beginning of another. And isn't that what death really is?

The success of the IST, combined with my self adopted relaxation routine (Taylor pre-flight) appears to be extremely promising. Who am I kidding? I am elated!

Soul Traveler

3

VISITATIONS

> "Experiences with projection of consciousness and knowledge of the mobility of consciousness are, therefore, very helpful as preparations for death.
> —Seth Speaks, Jane Roberts

23 October 93 (Tired)

I went to bed about 10:30 P.M. At 2:30 I got up, used the bathroom, and went back to bed. I Hu'd softly for a minute and relaxed.

☾ OBE BEGINS

My mind wandered until a musical tone quickly brought me to full awareness. The tone was not from any instrument I've ever heard. It was indescribable. I felt motion. I was floating upwards, and I could see the entire room. I looked around to see if anyone or anything was in the room with me. I was relieved there wasn't a third party. I mean. . .I was disappointed. Darn! I marveled at the experience for a moment, then I thought about going up to the roof.

As I went up through the ceiling, I thought of my body lying there in the bed. Suddenly I was back in my body with a bad case of the vibes. I thought about what had just happened. Then I turned my attention to floating upward. Shortly, I was on a collision course with the ceiling again. I marveled that I could make it happen.

I thought about visiting my friend Kim; and with that thought, I started to move toward the bedroom window. I was halfway though the glass, when the thought of my body entered my mind and with the blink of an eye, I was back in my body fully reconnected (able to move). I was determined to get out of body, so I attempted to disconnect once more. The next thing I knew I was driving my car.

Completely perplexed by the sudden shift in location, I asked myself over and over again, "Is this a dream?"

I thought about Doctor H. explaining that sometimes people create vehicles to move about during an OBE. After re-examining the situation, I thought of leaving the car while it was still moving. Whoops! Bad idea! I wasn't a hundred percent convinced I was having an OBE; this might be really happening. On the astral plane things self-generated appear to be as real as in the physical realm. I changed my mind and pulled the car over to the curb. For an astral vehicle the car was very responsive; easy to park too!

Without opening the door, I pushed through it and stood there next to my astral vehicle. As I turned my attention from it, the car became increasingly transparent and simply ceased to be. I stood there astonished.

I looked at my hands. They had an eerie glow around them. It was absolutely fascinating!

My entire "astral body" seemed to possess a soft luminescent quality. I looked at my surroundings and observed a nearby street corner. I asked mentally or telepathically to meet my guide on that corner. I then flew to the corner, but he/she/it was a no-show again. I mentally asked to meet the Mahanta, the Eckankar spiritual leader. I was told by an Eckist that Mahanta was capable of soul traveling at will. Members also told me if I wanted to see the Mahanta during soul travel, all I had to do was call him. Strike two! It's a good thing I was so apprehensive, otherwise I would have been disappointed.

I thought of my friend Kim again and was drawn up to the second floor of a nearby apartment building. I entered a kitchen through one of the walls. I looked around for a minute or two, feeling a lot like a cat burglar casing the joint. I felt a little uneasy and decided to make my exit through a window in one of the back bedrooms. It didn't occur to me that the apartment I was in might have been Kim's. For some reason that completely slipped my mind.

I dove out the window, turned left, and flew up the

alleyway. I decided to experiment with speed and altitude. I noticed that I was able to exercise better control over these two elements.

I thought of going back to my body and rapidly returned. At first I thought I'd reconnected, but I realized I had not.

I sat there halfway in and halfway out looking around the room for what seemed like a couple of minutes before I reconnected. I then raised my head and looked at the clock. It was 5:37 AM. I had been traveling for over three hours!

In earlier flights, before I found out that I was really having an OBE (I didn't know that it was by pure thought alone that I flew), a fearful thought would occur to me that I might lose altitude or fall; and immediately I would plummet from the sky in a panic. Most of the time I would pull back up just in the nick of time to skip across the ground, like a flat rock on a pond. I would then use my hands to push off the ground and climb skyward again. Other times I would fly at an extremely slow rate a few feet above the ground, unable to speed up or climb. All the while unbeknownst to me, my thoughts alone were the reason for these difficulties.

★ RETROSPECT

I have read that most dreams last only a few seconds or minutes, not usually hours. This was one of my first indications this was more than a dream. A week later, I thought about the apartment and how I arrived there by merely focusing my thoughts. I began to wonder if that was really Kim's apartment. I contacted Kim, and described the apartment to her with as much detail as I could remember. To my surprise, the apartment I described matched hers perfectly, even to the bedroom overlooking the alleyway. Later she sent me a floor plan of her place, and at once I knew I had been there. I was rapidly becoming a believer in the OBE phenomenon.

❧   ❧   ❧

7 November 93 (Average night)

Nothing special happened, but I did wake up during the night with a bad case of the vibes.

❧   ❧   ❧

10 November 93 (Average night)

I was dreaming when I became lucid to the extent that I was immediately back in my body and very much aware of the paralysis. I felt two hands pulling on my hips, as if someone was trying to help me get out of my body.

I projected mentally, "Stop it!" I reconnected. Nothing else happened.

★ RETROSPECT

All of this grabbing, touching, and pulling is a bit too much. Was still another entity trying to get me to "come out and play?" I could not help but wonder about its motives.

❧   ❧   ❧

14 November 93 (Restless, used the IST)

I went to bed and set the alarm for 2:30 AM. I got up when the alarm went off, stayed up for a short while, then went back to bed. I started to Hu softly. I lay there for some time. Nothing happened. Frustrated, I turned over on my side and fell asleep.

☾ OBE BEGINS

Suddenly I snapped to full consciousness observing that I was now floating above my bed. I must have been in a semi-dream state when I left my body. I decided to fly straight up through the roof. Who needs a door? As the upper part of my astral form penetrated the ceiling, I could see wooden cross beams and electrical wiring. I could also see six inches of fiberglass insulation between the attic floor and the roof. I always wondered about that!

When I pushed through the shingled roofing, I stared into an early morning sky filled with a multitude of tiny stars. I floated there above the roof of my house thoroughly amazed. I decided to try something a little different this time. Hovering there in the cool morning air, instantly the thought came to me. "I want to see the Light!" I projected. This Light that everyone in my metaphysical circle alluded to, as I understood it, has been described as an angel, Jesus, even God.

Well, maybe I got too cocky, because I was abruptly gripped with unexplainable fear. I felt panic setting in; I cried out for Rosanna, my friend from the IANDS meetings. Rosanna shared with me that two people having simultaneous OBEs could locate each other with very little difficulty. Suddenly, I was moving very rapidly and stopped just as abruptly.

I was standing in an apartment that was unfamiliar to me. Then all at once, without any warning, a rare thing happened. I lost consciousness and remember nothing after that point. I woke up that morning still visibly shaken from the unexplainable fear.

★ RETROSPECT

Could the apartment have been Rosanna's? Did I get in over my head? Was I too high, too fast, too soon? Needless to say, I knew that I needed to develop more confidence before I attempted to see the Light.

21 November 93 (Average night)

I performed my pre-flight routine and Hu'd softly. I was instantaneously aware of the paralysis along with the now familiar buzzing sound. I felt the upper half of my body begin to lift and float upward.

Like an advanced early warning radar system, my vision came on-line; although I was not quite ready to observe the humanoid shape standing on my right about three feet away. This time instead of panicking, I concentrated on the thought that this could be my Guide. I gathered all of the courage I had and said, "Hello." No response.

I repeated my greeting; still no answer! I was beginning to feel a little frightened having been given what I considered to be the "cold shoulder."

I gave up my attempts to communicate, reentered, and reconnected. I watched the figure slowly disappear as I completed the reconnection with my body.

☯   ☯   ☯

15 February 94 (Tired and relaxed)

I dropped off to sleep with my legs intertwined with Kathy's. I was jolted to full awareness by two sets of arms pulling on my astral arms. I also felt a great amount of pressure near my tail bone (coccyx).

I mentally projected that I didn't like that feeling, and the pressure immediately decreased but did not cease. I then reached up to feel the arms and hands that were pulling on me.

The arms were soft and feminine. I reconnected and opened my eyes. Kathy said I moaned aloud so she shook me with her legs.

★ **New information:** It is possible to have an OBE even though a human is physically touching me.

However, Doctor H. said that touching makes it difficult to have an OBE.

❧   ❧   ❧

21 February 94, Monday night (Nothing special)

Kathy was on a business trip, so I went to bed alone. Attempting an OBE without Kathy close by made me feel a little uneasy. I guess in a lot of ways I have grown astrally dependent on her. You might say Kathy is to me what an ejection seat is to a military jet pilot. When the situation gets out of control, with her help, I punch out. Not all of my OBEs have been planned; some have just happened. I wasn't sure if I was prepared for this possibility. I decided not to perform a pre-flight and drifted into a light sleep.

Shortly, I woke up in the paralysis. Since I was alone, I was very reluctant to "get out." I let go of the physical a little bit, then noticed that there were three to four humanoid figures standing around me. They appeared to have hoods and robes. I wasn't quite ready for this (as if I ever am!). I fought my way back to the physical and reconnected.

★ RETROSPECT

Oh, great! Who were the new apparitions? They resembled religious monks. I wondered if I was simply dreaming or was this an authentic visitation. And if so, what could they possibly want from me? I was really puzzled!

4

PSYCHIC RESCUE

14 March 94, Monday night (Nothing special)

I was dreaming that I was walking through my house when I woke up in the dream (became lucid). I was instantly back in my body in the paralysis, except in my third eye there was a picture. I focused on the picture, and it grew larger. Then I was in the picture. I leaned forward and took off into the sky. I flew around for awhile then returned back to my body. The picture in the third eye scenario reoccurred and I flew again but this time while flying, I felt drawn to a large one story building.

I floated through the front doors into a huge dining hall. The room was filled with humanoid figures dressed in eighteenth century attire. I immediately thought of "Gone with the Wind" and smiled, because I never liked that movie. Milling through the crowded room were three entities serving food and drinks. Although the room was filled to capacity, I somehow sensed these three shapes as the only genuine apparitions.

Feeling less threatened by the female entity, I cautiously approached her. She was dressed like the kitchen help from a southern plantation, circa 1800. The female looked at me, then quickly turned back to her duties. At first I pretended to talk to the figures at a nearby tables because I wasn't sure what was going on. Were these three figures entities or not? Why did I sense a difference between them and the rest of the figures? Why was I drawn here in the first place? Why did I feel the need to help them?

I watched the female entity for a while, then asked, "What are you doing?"

"Get back ta work!" she yelled, then moved away.

I approached her again and said, "You don't have to cater to these people anymore. They aren't real!"

"If'n you don't git back ta serv'in, you goan get whooped!"

I wondered for a moment who was going to administer this "whoop'in." I looked over at the two male apparitions, who fearfully glanced at me, then doubled their "serv'in" speed. I told the woman that I was leaving and that they were all welcome to come with me.

"We cain't do dat cuz they'll come after us!" blurted one of the males.

I turned to the seemingly crowded room and announced, "I'm leaving, and no one here's going to stop me!" (Where did all this courage come from?) The crowd of imitation people showed as much interest as a room full of mannequins. I walked to the front doors, went outside, and was immediately followed by all three of the entities I had been talking to.

"What we goan do now?" inquired the female.

"It's simple!" I said. "I will teach you how to fly!"

The four of us then headed down the street. One of the males kept looking back over his shoulder as if he expected an angry mob to suddenly burst from the building. Trying to ease his concerns, I turned to him and smiled. He seemed to sense my confidence and relaxed a bit. I instructed all of them to join hands, lean forward, and push off. We all flew! I kept the altitude low at first, then we began to climb rapidly.

I glanced back and forth checking on my students' progress. Suddenly without warning they disappeared.

★ RETROSPECT

I was bursting with questions about this encounter. Where did they disappear to? Why didn't I fear them as I usually do? How long had these three been stuck in this... pseudo-reality? Maybe two or three hundred years? I remember Doctor H. explaining when people die they sometimes become prisoners in their own self-created belief system. For example, an individual may pass on and not know it, or refuse to accept his own death, then he may continue to "haunt" an old stomping ground, castle, hotel, etc.

(Note: I would not understand this enigma for several months to come.)

I became curious about the origin of the expression the "Witches are Riding You." I have been told this was used to describe the paralysis by my grandmother's generation.

My aunt informed me that she has a book which describes witches traveling out of body. She told me that she was reading the book and became so frightened that she tossed the book up into the top of her closet and tried to forget it. The book remained there unopened for years.

Well, to make a long story short, I got my eager little hands on this mystical manuscript and studied it enthusiastically. The title of the book was *The Magic of Witchcraft*.

The book described how witches were linked with the dead and astral travel and how they communicated with spirits while OBE. Bingo! The book also explains how witches lingered around graveyards to assist the newly departed dead to adapt to the spirit realm.

It appears that witches have taken on the responsibility of rescuing lost souls from their own self-imposed pseudo-realities. Was this what I did on March 14, 1994? Could I be considered a witch? The witches call this task "psychic rescue." I began to wonder if this is how the paralysis became associated with "riding witches?" Was it merely a coincidence that witches also practiced astral travel? Was some long lost secret finally coming to light?

Three hundred years ago would I have been accused of practicing witchcraft? Were early astral travelers burned at the stake in Salem for speaking of their OBE explorations? An interesting connection is that this theory of "psychic rescue" is described in the book *Seth Speaks* and in Robert Monroe's last book *Ultimate Journey*.

This then explains the compelling urge I had to help the southern plantation entities. Is this what I am supposed to be doing as part of my OBE travels? Am I destined to help lost and confused souls? Is this part of the universal plan that the Creator has established? If it is, then I feel very fortunate to be a part of it.

I began to wonder if this could now explain my fear of ghosts and spirits. Have they been trying to contact me unbeknownst to my personality self? Am I in some sort of training to become a "spirit guide?" I can't help but think of the wondrous possibilities.

In early September 1994, I had an interesting short OBE that might backup my newly adopted theory about my role as a psychic rescuer. After lying down and performing a quicker relaxation routine I've labeled the abbreviated pre-flight, I drifted off to sleep.

☾ OBE BEGINS

Dreaming...dreaming...slight awareness, I could hear a voice...I snapped to full consciousness. I was in a crowd of forty or fifty non-physical beings. Confused and disoriented I asked myself, "Is this a dream?" This crowd of entities all focused on a single being toward the front and slightly above everyone else. No one paid any attention to me. I was just part of the spiritual audience.

The "speaker" said all beings present were a part of a particular purpose. I couldn't control my emotions and became overly excited. Was I in a class for astral travelers? Were these beings disembodied spirits or were they like me, spiritual tourists? The excitement over-powered me, and I could feel myself being forced to return to my body. I released and gave in. I immediately returned and sat up in bed astonished at this new piece to my puzzle.

❧ ❧ ❧

5 April 94, 9:45 P.M. (Angels on the brain)

That night I went to bed asking aloud for help in having a conscious OBE. I performed the Taylor pre-flight, lay flat on my back, and drifted off into a light sleep.

☾ OBE BEGINS

I was instantly in the paralysis. I also observed that Kathy was holding my hand; at least I thought it was her. I noticed the hand felt smaller than usual, almost childlike. I felt my astral body floating upward from the waist down. I projected, "I don't want to have an OBE." Fear had changed my mind.

A male voice then spoke into my left ear, and I had to calm my fear. The voice changed to female as if it sensed my fear. The female voice was more calming but not much. As if to further ease my anxiety, the voice changed to a soft whisper. I found this less threatening, and I tried to relax. But I still didn't want an OBE, soft voice or not!

This conflict continued for several hours. I would force myself to reconnect with my physical body, only to start drifting out again. I reconnected and sat up. Kathy was over on the other side of our king size bed. Her back and hands were out of my reach. So, whose hand have I been holding? I lay down and swiftly slipped back into the paralysis. The hand was there again, gently holding mine.

After I forced another earthly reconnection, I got out of

bed, walked into the bathroom and said aloud, "That is enough; I have got to go to work!"

I looked at the clock, alarmed to see it was 1:00 AM. The whole series of events had taken three hours! I went back to bed and slept the remainder of the night without further interruption.

Over the past few months I have found that I am developing a hunger for metaphysical literature. I read everything I can find. The odd thing is that most of the books I have read have been gifts or have been recommended by a friend, or sometimes by a complete stranger.

One occasion, after eating breakfast at a local restaurant and waiting at the cash register to pay my tab, a man commented about the book I was holding.

"That's a good book," he said. The book was *Seth Speaks* by Jane Roberts.

"I know," I said. "I can't seem to put it down."

He asked, "Have you read *Visions* by Wilkerson?"

"No, I haven't," I said.

"Get it!" He smiled and walked out.

One book referral in particular still remains a mystery. I attended the monthly IANDS meeting with Doctor H. At the good doctor's insistence, I found myself sitting in the middle of a room describing a recent OBE. After I finished speaking, one of the IANDS members walked up to me and slipped a piece of paper into my shirt pocket. He said, "This is your next book!"

I looked at the paper; it read *Zolar's Encyclopedia of Ancient and Forbidden Knowledge*. It wasn't the most exciting or inviting title I'd ever heard, but what the heck! The next day I ordered the book.

12 April 94 (Average night nothing special)

I was lying down and going through the "Taylor pre-flight." I let go of the physical. I don't remember leaving my body, but I do recall the sensation of flying. I seemed to be on "auto-pilot," flying high and steady.

I remembered I had spoken to an Eck friend about my failed attempts to meet my guide. My friend asked simply, "Did you look behind you?"

I decided to take advantage of the auto-pilot condition, and I looked back over my shoulders, toward the back of my legs.

Oh my God! To my surprise there was an "entity" supporting my legs and feet helping me to fly! I waved at *It* and *It* waved back. This was weird! It released my legs, flew up beside me, and hugged my waist. Fear gripped me, but I managed to suppress it. The entity pointed downward at what looked like Stonehenge. We circled repeatedly over this ancient cathedral. I could see figures moving in and around the huge stones. Each would stop briefly at a pillar, then move on to the next.

This scene reminded me of patrons at an art gallery. The entity/guide began to tell me something about this famous attraction. I concentrated so hard on controlling my fear, that I missed what the entity said. I felt I'd had enough of this new experience and thought of returning to my body. I sensed a sudden, quick, visual shift, then rapid motion. I was back and reconnected. I felt very disturbed by what I'd just seen!

19 April 94 (Average night nothing special)

I prepared for take-off, relaxed, and let go of my physical body.

ᴄ OBE BEGINS

I found myself flying in "auto-pilot" mode again. I looked over my shoulder, and there was my auto-pilot. This time "Otto" (as in "Otto-matic pilot") did not wait for me to acknowledge his presence. Otto flew up next to me, and hugged me around my waist. I didn't want to look at Otto directly, but I did notice his color and skin pattern kept changing.

Once again Otto pointed down. We were flying over Stonehenge. The fear crept over me as Otto spoke into my ear. I still cannot recall what Otto said. We flew round and round over Stonehenge. Otto continued to speak. I was uneasy. I decided to return. I thought of my body, there was a quick shift, I reconnected and sat up. Although I tried, I was not able to go back to sleep!

★ RETROSPECT

Until that point every OBE I'd experienced was unique; there had been no repeat trips.

A week later I received a phone call from the bookstore. *Zolar* had arrived and I could pick it up. I drove to the bookstore in Newport Beach, walked in, asked for the book, paid for it, and left. I walked through the parking lot toward my car carrying the book. *Zolar* was thoroughly wrapped in brown paper. I tore off the paper and was shocked by the cover—a picture of Stonehenge covered the book. Remembering my last two OBEs, I began to feel a weird tingling sensation creeping up my spine. What the heck was this about?

20 September 94 (Tired sleepy)

I went to bed at 9:15 and dropped off immediately. I was awake at 1:28 to use the bathroom. Back in bed, I couldn't fall asleep. I tossed and turned until 4:12, when finally something began to happen. My body slowly fell asleep as the paralysis took over.

☾ OBE BEGINS

My legs began to rise upwards. I wanted to sit up, and I did. Sitting felt so natural that I had to make sure that I didn't sit up physically. I stood up and noticed my feet touched the carpet. I walked over to the foot of the bed. As I walked, I simply thought about floating, and I did!

I thought about walking on the carpet, and I floated down and walked. Amazing!! I floated over to the mirror on the back of the bedroom door and noticed I had no reflection. *Count Dracula, eat your heart out!*

I put my hand through the mirror on the back of the bedroom door, paused, then dove through it into the hallway. I floated there trying to decide where I should go. Kim came to mind, and I focused on her. Without warning, I felt two hands on either side of me gently grabbing my arms. The hands turned me around and pushed/pulled me out through the wall. I saw nothing but blackness. Then I stood in front of an apartment building. I was totally disoriented. Confused, I forgot my destination. Does this sound familiar? I decided to call for Otto, again. I pointed to a spot ten feet away and said, "Please appear over there." I looked behind me, but no Otto. Well, being ignored by a non-physical being plays havoc with one's ego! I then began to think of my body, experienced a quick visual shift, felt a slight bit of movement, was back, and reconnected.

★ RETROSPECT

For some reason my memory fails me in the astral body, I sometimes forget where I am going.

Thought processing appears to be quite different during soul traveling, almost as if a data link with the brain has been interrupted. It appears that people, places, and things with which I have no emotional ties are of little significance.

If I planned, while in the physical state, to soul travel to a foreign country to observe top secret activities, this event would likely not occur. Not because I am incapable of doing it, but for the reason that it has no spiritual significance. While soul traveling, I wonder if I think more like the spiritual being that I am, rather than the earthly personality self I've slipped free of?

Soul Traveler

5

A CHANGE IN PERSPECTIVE

Truly, I would be remiss in my obligations to the reader if I did not describe the lasting affects the OBEs and metaphysical literature has had on me. During and after the OBE on April 3, 1993, several impressions have become a permanent part of my consciousness.

I no longer have a fear of death, not that I dwelled on it before—it has merely lost its finality. I believe there is a hereafter, and whatever defines me as me will consciously survive. My relationship with IANDS and Rosanna has strengthened this belief tremendously. I have heard numerous first hand accounts of near death experiences and to me they appear to be relative to my jaunts. However, I have not died! And, unlike what I have heard about the near death experience, I seem to have more control over my travels. I choose where to go and when to return . . . most of the time. I also have what I describe as a "knowing" that has stayed with me since the OBE April 3, 1993. I am convinced that the lack of a physical body is my timeless natural state, and existing with a physical body is as temporary as a dream.

During the April 1993 OBE, I had an overwhelming feeling of being home, at last. This feeling has confused me, because I don't have any conscious memories to substantiate it.

My current relationships with everyone—close relatives, friends, and strangers—are more open, honest, and caring—unlike anything I've previously thought probable. My wife and friends have repeatedly referred to me as "a spiritual guide." I take this as a great compliment, although I don't agree. I have shared my insights into problems or self-defeating behavior with others that seems to have helped them.

Sometimes my suggestion would be a different way of looking at a situation. The strangest part about the suggestions (or insights) is I have no idea where the information comes from. In most cases, the guidance I've offered is news to me too! I do not make predictions or anything of that sort; just observations that appear to be very clear to me.

On several occasions I have applied the new insights to my own life with positive results. This remains an enigma . . . at least to me.

★ **New Information:** I have found my worst enemy during OBEs to be my own uncontrolled imagination. I have learned that whatever I imagine—devils, demons, or pink elephants—will be created instantly. I have found that it is important to keep my thoughts clear and uncluttered.

In addition, it is important not to prejudge or guess what is going to happen, because I might be the one creating it! It is important to keep dreamlike manifestations from contaminating my OBEs. But controlled use of the imagination during an OBE can be quite amazing and down right fun! I wonder if most OBEs are camouflaged by self-created dream material. During the paralysis, the power to create is still available. In some instances I have chosen to create a dream rather than leave the body . . . but not often.

Earlier in the year I was invited by my friend Kim to explore my imagination in a slightly different manner. Kim invited me to attend a past life regression experiment conducted by a prominent hypnotherapist in Newport Beach, California. At this point I was open to practically anything.

My relationship with Kim is a little on the unusual side, almost like a sister. This I find strange, because I have no siblings and have never wished for any. But there is a bond that has been apparent to me from our initial meeting. So, when I drove to Newport Beach, I was asking myself over and over again, "Why are you doing this? This is a waste of time and money. Turn around while you still can! What does this have to do with OBEs anyway?"

I arrived, and Kim drove up shortly thereafter. Kim explained how she'd done this before with remarkable results. We walked to a nearby house, knocked on the door and a middle-aged woman opened the door and greeted us with a smile.

"Welcome! I'm Dr. Carbone," she said, then turned for us to follow. "We are just about to get started." She grinned as we climbed the staircase.

As I followed behind Kim, I couldn't help but notice a sign which read, "This house is protected by ghosts!" Instantly, I was ready to leave!

We entered a small but cozy den with six other people already seated. We exchanged greetings, then found our seats. Kim and I were seated on opposite ends of the room. I felt a little silly and sat there staring at Kim.

Dr. Carbone explained to us what was to come and that we should relax and follow her instructions.

A Change in Perspective

The doctor started a tape of prerecorded music and began to lead us toward a light hypnotic state. I sat there relaxing my body with relative ease, almost like performing a pre-flight. Then the thought occurred to me, "I hope I don't . . . pop out!"

After ensuring that the participants were thoroughly relaxed, she began to describe a forest with tall swaying trees. In the forest she described a long, winding path and directed us to follow it. At the end of the path was a house— one that we lived in during a past life.

Having what I considered to be an active imagination, I gave into her prompting and made an effort to visualize this abode. In my mind's eye, I pictured a white and brown German cottage with darker brown shutters. Following her guidance I moved to the door, opened it, and walked in. I could see a half circular staircase on the left and a dining area toward the right.

I moved to the dining table and observed the pewter dishes neatly placed. I marveled at all of this because Dr. Carbone stopped verbally directing us after I entered the doorway.

I was pleased because my imagination was better than I'd thought. I noticed a warm, flickering glow radiating from the fireplace. I turned and walked over to the staircase. I climbed quickly and entered one of the bedrooms at the top of the stairs. Inside the room on the left wall was a closet which stood out from the wall and was supported by short wooden legs. I opened the closet and it was filled with women's clothes. Then a strange feeling swept over me. I had an instinctive impression that the clothes were . . . mine! This was getting too weird.

Dr. Carbone cut in, "You are leaving that life through a long tunnel. As you emerge on the other side, you will be in a life previous to the one we just visited."

I was now standing on a snow-covered mountain side. Tall trees dotted the sides of the hills. There was smoke from camp fires permeating the air. But there was something else. People were moaning. No, people were dying. No, *my* people were dying. *We* were starving! I looked down at my feet which were covered by furry, knee-high, crudely crafted boots.

This was too much! Was my imagination really that good? I looked up from my boots to see some of the dead being carried away on two parallel sticks, drawn by horses. Then it suddenly hit me. My people were dying because the Cavalry had driven us away from our home land and into the mountains.

"I want you to go to the last day of that life," Dr. Carbone interceded.

I was suddenly lying there covered by thick furs. I felt that I was mortally wounded during a very one-sided battle. We had returned to fight for our land—the land of my father, and the land of my father's father.

We didn't have a chance and were brutally slaughtered. I looked around and saw that I was in a circular pointed room with a fire burning in the center. A flap of hide at the top was partially open to let the rising smoke escape. I...

"At the count of five, I want you to return to this life," Dr. Carbone interrupted. "You are healthy and whole."

"One . . . two . . . three . . . four . . . ," I sat up slowly thinking, "What a great imagination I have." Like the dead coming back to life, the other time travelers began to stretch and yawn.

Dr. Carbone looked straight at me and said, "So, tell us about your experience. Did anything happen?"

"Uh, no. That's all right; I was just using my imagination." (Wasn't I?)

"Please, don't be shy. Tell us!" insisted Dr. Carbone, prying away my defenses.

Reluctantly I shared my story, but only included bits and pieces with very little detail. While I spoke, I couldn't help but notice Kim staring at me with a blank look and her mouth wide open. "What's with her?" I thought. I didn't think my story was THAT interesting.

I quickly ended my fairy tale and relinquished the podium. The good doctor thanked me for sharing, then began interrogating the next person. Kim was still staring at me! Did I make a fool out of myself? I started to feel uncomfortable. It didn't take long for the doctor to begin asking Kim about her experiences. Kim finally stopped staring and started talking.

Kim began to tell the exact same story as mine. While

I listened, I began to feel very disappointed in Kim. Why would she blatantly plagiarize my imaginary story? Was she trying to give my story some validity, to keep me from regretting this entire venture? Was I that transparent? I was trying to hide my doubts about coming here in the first place.

She began to describe the table settings inside the cottage. She spoke of the radiant fire and the large wooden dining table.

Wait a minute! I didn't share that part of the story! Was this just a lucky guess? What was she up to? I began to wonder if the rest of the people were in on the joke. This couldn't have been all arranged for my benefit, could it? No, this is far too elaborate. Kim then began to describe her reincarnated life prior to the German one.

I couldn't believe that she was trying to pull another fast one. She began to describe the snow scene in the mountains but from a slightly different perspective. How clever of her to try to make her story credible by changing the perspective. She continued to describe the scene, the starvation, the dead being dragged off on two sticks.

Hold on a minute! I completely left that part out! My mouth dropped open! I quickly found myself staring at her waiting for a slip-up in her testimony. Kim continued to describe events and details that I did not share but imagined. I was at a loss.

After the entire session ended Kim and I continued to collaborate our experiences, which shocked both of us. "I don't believe in reincarnation!" I said. "At least I thought I didn't!"

Was there some logical explanation? How could we share the same . . . daydream? Kim began to tell me how more times than not, souls somehow reincarnate together lifetime after lifetime. Well, I never would have guessed that I could leave my body and fly all over creation. Maybe reincarnation is possible. Maybe anything is possible!

June 94 (sleepy)

I woke up in the paralysis and, without my prodding, the lower half of my body began to float.

★ OBE BEGINS:

I could feel my astral body moving upward. Like the hinged lid of a music box, my astral body moved up and my head rotated backwards! The soles of my astral feet were pointing straight at the ceiling. I was upside down and facing backwards, but my astral head was still connected to my physical head. I hung there upside down staring at the headboard of our bed. I couldn't seem to break free, gave up, and reconnected.

August 94 (IST)

I performed an abbreviated pre-flight and teetered on the edge of sleep. Still in my physical body I snapped to full lucidity having been startled by the sound of a roaring wind.

☾ OBE BEGINS:

While basking in the paralysis, I decided to choose a destination before I left my body. I thought of flying near the clouds, then something very different occurred. I faded or dissolved out of my body and materialized flying high above the ground. That was different! I paused, then reached for the sky, and climbed at an incredible rate of speed. Soon I was among the clouds. Most were heavily saturated with moisture. I was homing in on a large dark cloud when my internal warning system went off. A peculiar feeling of danger took hold of me which confused me. But one thing was clear, change course, now! I increased the astral throttle and went ballistic! Suddenly there were no clouds, just an endless night filled with tiny points of light. It was beautiful! All around me were twinkling stars. I was mesmerized!

The moon seemed to be rushing toward me. Incredible! I veered off and turned back toward the Earth. I could hardly contain myself. I could see the Earth's oceans and land masses through a cloudy veil.

I kept asking myself why hadn't I done this before? The land was rapidly approaching. Down, down, down . . .

A Change in Perspective

I was falling! I screeched to a halt high above the ground, paused, and assured myself I was still in control. No malfunctions, and all systems go! I dove downward again, aiming towards the west coastline of North America.

As I approached the coast of California, I could see the faint lines of highways and roads. Soon I could see cities and clumps of buildings. I flew in low over a street. I could see cars. People were crossing streets or standing at bus stops. I flew up to a street sign, and floated there, staring at the sign. I could not read the words. I could see letters or symbols but nothing more. I felt astrally dyslexic. If I had to find my way home using visual flight rules, I would probably never return and become a mystery like Amelia Earhart. I decided to perform a quick shift to simplify returning. I focused my thoughts on my body, felt the shift from location to location, reconnected, and opened my physical eyes. This excursion for me was a giant leap astrally.

Soul Traveler

6

My Body
and Me

Early May 94, 9:40 P.M. (Feeling calm and confident)

I zipped right through the pre-flight; all systems were go; I released the physical.

☾ OBE BEGINS

The paralysis crept over me, forcing gravity to release its

grip. I was immediately aware of a loud roaring sound all around me. It was as if a wind storm raged in my bedroom. The noise was almost too much to bear.

My upward motion suddenly came to an abrupt halt. As if from nowhere, someone or something pressed firmly up against my backside. From the back of my head to the heels of my feet, someone was there. I projected mentally, "Otto, I don't like this!" No response. "Who are you?" I inquired, and still no response. I reached back with my astral hands, and felt down a pair of arms until I reached the hands. I grabbed the hands and shook them trying to provoke a reaction, to no avail. The hands felt lifeless and rubbery. The hands and fingers were oddly flattened and tucked in close to its legs.

This "thing" was not only pressed hard against me, but it was breathing slowly in my ear, and I didn't like it. If this thing is Otto, then he's showing far too much affection for me. My fear immediately sprang into action, and I hit the panic button. Abort...abort...abort!

Nothing happened! Where was Kathy? Didn't she hear me? I suddenly remembered telling her if she heard me moan, don't touch me, because I can reconnect...all by *myself*! I panicked and completely forgot about the "little finger" trick. I hit the alarm again, and no response. I felt a hard shove, reconnected with my body, and sprang to a sitting position.

"Didn't you hear me!" I exclaimed.

"You said you could handle it by yourself!" she

mocked, then turned over and went back to sleep.

I got up and walked into the bathroom still visibly shaken. I looked into the mirror, and I immediately knew what had transpired during the OBE. The "thing" was my own body! I remembered tucking my hands in close to my thighs as part of my pre-flight preparations. And the slow deep breathing made sense for a sleeping person/body.

I went back to bed feeling a little foolish. Being afraid of my own body was one reason; the other was the overconfidence that Kathy pointed out for me. Enough said, lesson learned.

10 May 94 (Average evening, tired)

I lay down not really thinking OBE, relaxed and drifted off to sleep.

☾ OBE BEGINS

I woke at the sound of an intermittent loud crackling. I was vibrating like crazy! I prepared for lift-off, focused my thoughts, and rose majestically upward into the...ceiling fan! I stopped and quickly looked back at the bed.

In the bed lay two figures, one of them me? Until this OBE, I have avoided looking directly at my body. I'm not really sure why, but I looked this time, briefly.

Kathy was on her left side with her back toward my body. It was strange how detached I felt looking at what was supposed to be me. But yet it wasn't really me at all; more like a costume I wear. I moved over to a corner and quickly scanned the room looking for uninvited guests. I saw no entities in the room. But something was different. No, I was different. I was not using my astral body. I was not using any body at all!

I can describe this in no other way but this: I appeared to be a pin point of consciousness and nothing else. I could see the room in all directions, at once! Where was my astral body? Did I forget it somewhere? I was overwhelmed, amazed, and ready to return. I floated back to my body without incident and reconnected. I sat up and reached for my journal that I'd begun to keep. This could not wait!

★ RETROSPECT

What was this all about? I seemed to have left my astral body behind. I have begun to wonder why I needed an astral body in the first place.

Could it be that the shock of not having a body would be too disorienting? Did a part of me, maybe the higher self, create the vehicle to provide some stability for my consciousness?

7

YOU'RE NEVER TOO OLD

> *"We can lift ourselves out of ignorance, we can find ourselves as creatures of excellence, intelligence and skill. We can be free! We can learn to fly!"*
>
> **—Richard Bach,**
> **Jonathan Livingston Seagull**

In all my excitement about OBEs, I completely forgot that my mother still suffered with the paralysis. At the age of 72, I wondered if she too can have an OBE. If nothing else, I can relieve her concerns about what happened to Robert . . . can't I?

"The witches are riding you!" is how my grandmother described it. Would my mother's fear of this prevent her

71

from "getting out?" I sat with my mother and shared some of my discoveries about the paralysis.

Surprisingly enough, she was very receptive and actually eager to perform some of her own experiments. A week or two later my mother told me the following:

"I woke up paralyzed and nearly forced my way out of it," she said. "I then thought about what you said and relaxed a bit." She then repeated several times, "I want to float upwards." She told me as she began to rise, she became aware of someone holding her hand. (I had not shared with her my OBE on April 5, 1994 when I too had found myself holding a mystery hand.) Unlike me she was not fearful, even though this was her first flight. She did, however, feel uncomfortable outside of her body and quickly returned.

In the later part of 1994, I spoke with my cousin Robert's wife, Catherine. She explained to me that they were married for 32 years, and Robert had the witches "riding" him for the entire time. One of the ultimate opportunities knocked on Robert's door, and he was afraid to answer. Or should I say, he did not know how to answer it! With a description like "the witches are riding," who would want to answer? Catherine later shared with me a story that I believe shows just how close he may have been.

One morning Catherine woke early and left the bedroom leaving Robert still sleeping in their bed. Their granddaughter, Denise, was visiting and rose from bed early as well. Denise, eager to see if her grandfather was awake, walked into the bedroom and crept over to the bed. "Poppi," as she called him, was lying there with his eyes closed, repeatedly moaning. Thinking Robert was dreaming, she left without disturbing him. Catherine heard the barely audible moaning and looked away from the television to see Denise slipping out of the bedroom.

"What is that noise?" she asked the child.

"Oh, that's just Poppi making that noise," Denise said innocently.

Catherine realized that the moaning was Robert's signal to be shaken awake, ran into the bedroom, and shook Robert frantically. Robert woke and immediately complained.

"That child came into the room, looked into my face, and left without waking me!"

"She didn't know you wanted to be awakened," defended Catherine. I find it interesting that Denise saw her grandfather lying there asleep, which infers that his eyes were closed. He spoke of her walking into the room, looking at him, then leaving. Could Robert have been peering at her through his third eye? How could he see Denise at all? Was he slightly "out of body?"

Catherine told me that not only did Robert have a problem with riding witches; but also his father, his brother and even their daughter.

"Your daughter?" I asked very interested.

"Yes, Catty still suffers from that problem," she replied. I could hardly contain my excitement. There was someone else, with whom I could share my discovery. I asked for Catty's address, phone number, thanked Catherine, and left.

Later that week I met with Catty, who was fifty-two-years-young, and shared practically everything I could remember about my OBEs. With enthusiasm I told her that she too could soon be off on her own excursions. With eager anticipation I sat there waiting for her to respond to my fervor. After listening to me for a half hour or so, she gazed at me with a rigor mortis-like expression and remarked, "Why would I want to do that? I just want to know how to reconnect."

I was snatched back to reality! Just because OBEs have become a major part of my life, why would I assume it would be for her too? I shared with her the "little finger trick," apologized for taking up so much of her time, and left.

It hadn't occurred to me that a person who had the paralysis might not be interested in out of body experiences. From that point on I decided to be a little more cautious in talking about OBEs.

8

A RELATIVE ENCOUNTER

> *"Life is a state of becoming, and death is merely a part of the process."*
> — *Seth Speaks,* **Jane Roberts**

Mid 1994, during one of my OBE flights, I was drawn to a location I can only describe as "a meeting place." I do not believe this place is a physical location. If it is, it's not on Earth. On two occasions I have felt an irresistible urge to "blink out" and follow its magnetic pull. When in this location I felt overwhelmed by the countless entities seemingly milling around. These beings paid very little if any attention to me.

I wondered if this was an entity's self-created pseudo-reality, or was I in the midst of hundreds of entities? Remarkably I only felt a little fearful. I scanned the crowd and was puzzled as to why they were here, wherever here was. Suddenly, I recognized the face of a being a short distance away—looking directly at me! I thought, "No way; it couldn't be her." The entity bore a striking resemblance to my late Aunt Vera. Why would I see her? I haven't thought of her in years. I almost never think of her.

My Aunt Vera was my mother's sister who died of cancer in August 1982. I was very close to Aunt Vera in my youth, but we had grown distant during most of my adult life.

Now here is my aunt, standing/floating directly in front of me. I felt fear rear its ugly head. If this is her, then she is the first spirit I knew who lived and died in my lifetime. I was a pallbearer at her funeral! This encounter unleashed a flood of emotions that I simply could not handle. I thought of my body and retreated for home, at warp speed. When I reconnected I was dazed by what had occurred.

Should I tell my mother I saw her deceased youngest sister? Was it really her? She did appear to recognize/notice me, while the other beings paid no attention.

A few days later I slipped free of my body and took off

on a local sortie. Soon there was the magnetic pull I experienced before. I followed it. I arrived to observe the multitudes similar as before. This time I had one person on my mind, my aunt. As if responding to a page, there, a short distance away, was Aunt Vera. Only this time she was slowly approaching me.

With two parts courage and one part fear, I curiously inquired, "Aunt Vera, aren't you dead?"

"Yes, I am!" she said smiling at me.

I stared at her in partial disbelief. Yes it was her—a part of me knew it. I also could feel an intense sensation of love emanating from her. It was wonderful! I returned the feeling without hesitation.

I felt a need to return to my body, focused my thoughts, and sped off. After reconnecting, I reflected on what had occurred and realized the ever present fear of spirits had diminished dramatically. I understood a little more about them somehow and was comforted.

In early October 1994 Kathy and I had been following her uncle's progress after surviving surgery which removed a grapefruit-sized tumor from his chest. Kathy's Uncle Bill was now in critical condition in a Los Angeles hospital. On October 7th, at 10:15 pm, the phone rang once. Kathy answered. By the sound of Kathy's voice, I knew the inevitable had happened. Bill was no longer a physical being; he was free from suffering at last.

I comforted Kathy the best I could, until she drifted off to sleep. I relaxed beside her and wondered if it was too soon to attempt an encounter with Bill. Was it even possible? I decided to try and focused my thoughts on him as much as I could. I performed an abbreviated pre-flight, relaxed, and released.

☾ OBE BEGINS

Shortly thereafter I was aware of the detachment which signals the presence of the paralysis.

I allowed the upper half of my astral body to rise slightly above the physical. Suddenly I felt the approach of a presence just beyond the bedroom door. The presence was strong and unmistakable; someone was definitely approaching.

I stared as a humanoid figure stood motionless in the doorway of our bedroom. I could hardly control myself. Was Bill paying us a visit, or was it...a burglar?

I instantly reconnected, and sat up physically. The doorway was vacant and all was well. I laid back down, I had hopes of returning to the paralysis, and quickly did. I rose above the physical again, and there was the apparition part way through the doorway.

Oh my God! Is this her uncle? And if it isn't, then who else could it be? I could not make out the facial features. Even if I could, I might not have recognized him because I'd only seen Bill a couple of times. But, seemingly at my request, his spirit was paying us a visit.

The entity slowly backed away from the doorway, and I could no longer feel its presence. I reconnected, sat up, and reached for my journal. At that point I became a believer in the OBE phenomenon!

The encounters with my aunt and Kathy's uncle remind me of the second phenomena involving my father I alluded to in the introduction of this book.

On March 15, 1973, I was an Airman First Class in the United States Air Force, stationed in Wichita Falls, Texas. Having been born and raised in California, I felt like a fish out of water there. To escape from our unfamiliar surroundings, a few fellow servicemen and I decided to spend a day at Six Flags Over Texas, an amusement park.

We all boarded the largest roller coaster and prepared for the worst. About half way through the ride a feeling unlike anything I've ever felt consumed me. Overwhelming sadness and depression dominated me totally. I could no longer enjoy the remainder of the ride. When I exited the coaster, my friends became immediately aware of my mood.

"Are you okay, Al? You don't look so good!"

"I'm alright, but something is very wrong. Something has happened; I can feel it!" I said.

Nothing made sense, I was supposed to be having a good time, not depressing everyone. But the feeling that gripped me was not to be ignored.

"I have to call my mother in Los Angeles!" I blurted out. I found a public phone and called home. My mother answered the phone; and without pausing to say hello, I desperately inquired, "Mom what's wrong?"

My mother replied, "Albert we have been trying to contact you most of the day. Your father just died!"

It was as if a subconscious part of me sensed a problem, and the conscious part of me knew were to find the answer. The overpowering sadness that I felt made sense now. I shared the sad news with my friends.

"That was weird, Al! How did you know?"

"I have no idea!" I replied. "No idea."

Later that day, I returned to the place I was living just outside of Sheppard Air Force Base. As we pulled up I noticed a note flapping back and forth on the windshield of my car. It was from the Red Cross, stating that it was urgent and that I should contact them at once. I called the number on the note, sure of its purpose.

After arriving back in Los Angeles, I found out more about my father's passing. Although being repeatedly warned by his physician, my father died from the highly practiced disease of alcoholism. He drank himself to death.

In July 1994, after having experienced what was becoming a series of supernatural encounters, I decided to explore the world of ghosts. In the last two years I have attended numerous lectures and classes on esoteric subjects such as mind projection, psycho-kinetic energy

A Relative Encounter

(spoon bending), opening your "third eye," lucid dreaming, and ghost hunting. The majority of these were held at a reputable facility known as The Learning Light Foundation in Anaheim, California.

Having attended these classes, I signed up to receive the monthly newsletter. In a few months I received an edition which featured an internationally known psychic and medium. Rose Clifford was said to have acquired, at the age of sixteen, the capability to communicate with the spirit world. She was now 52-years-young. Reflecting back, I would have scoffed at mediums or psychics, but the recent events had permanently changed all that.

I made an appointment to see this evidential medium (whatever that is); and, because of her popularity, I had to make my appointment two weeks in advance. During the next two weeks, I kept telling myself I was not going to tell the medium anything that might give her material to develop a script.

Two weeks passed, and I soon found myself shaking hands with the medium who greeted me with a staunch British accent. She motioned for me to sit facing her, then asked to hold my wedding ring. Saying nothing at all, I smiled and handed my ring to her.

The medium waited all of two minutes then stated, "There is a man here, a tall man." (Okay, that's pretty generic.)

"You were his boy," she relayed. (This was beginning to sound a little rehearsed.)

"He says he is sorry he left you." (Well I guess I wasted my time and money!)

"Oh, this man drank a bit didn't he?" (I began to focus on her again, but still gave no response.)

"As a matter of fact, his drinking is what killed him." (She had my full attention, although she did not specifically say it was my father.)

"There is also a grandfather here. He appears to have had a drinking problem too." (This was truth about my mother's father, but she was still too ambiguous.)

"That's very interesting," I finally said.

"I also sense that you are being influenced by or have been in contact with one or two beings of light," she inserted. (Was she referring to Otto and company?)

The medium said she saw me speaking at a podium before a large crowd of people. I did not know it then, but two months later I would be asked to speak at a popular men's club to a group of 100 or more. Although I tried to foil her prediction and decline the offer, the scheduled speaker developed a severe throat infection, which left me without a way out. During the entire hour lecture I kept thinking back to Ms. Clifford's unescapable prophesy.

9

STAR LIGHT, STAR BRIGHT

> *"With God all things are possible."*
> **—Matthew 19:26**

The astral body is a wondrous vehicle. It provides a sense of security and stability for the personality self, by emulating the physical body. It allows us to appear well dressed, beautiful, handsome, and as tall or short as our ego wants us to be. But the astral body is not always needed. I believe it is just one more costume we wear. It appears to serve the same purpose as a child's security blanket. What the soul would look like visually without the astral body is definitely beyond my present comprehension.

๑ ๑ ๑

31 October 1994, Halloween night (Meditated for 20 minutes)

I fell asleep with my hand on Kathy's leg. Shortly thereafter I was yanked back to full awareness and very much conscious of the paralysis.

☾ OBE BEGINS

I sat up astrally and surveyed the bedroom—no third party. I moved to my left toward Kathy in a backward sliding motion. I was dragging something behind me which felt like a deflated inner-tube.

Suddenly I realized that parts of me were in three separate locations. My physical body was flat on its back on the right side of our bed. My astral body was the deflated inner tube dragging behind me, and the *I* that was *me* was a pin point of consciousness. I surveyed all of this in complete bewilderment.

I continued to move around Kathy's head and to my amazement I was not my normal size. I was tiny and Kathy appeared to be a giant! I slid to Kathy's left side staring at her with childlike curiosity, when she suddenly moved. As if I were at the end of my leash, I was instantaneously jerked back into my bodies. I reconnected and realized that my physical hand was still resting on

Kathy's leg. Every time she moved, so would my hand. This forced me to return to my body, or should I say bodies. I lay back trying not to move and mentally reached out for the paralysis which responded almost immediately. I detached from the physical and sat up astrally.

Otto stood on my right toward the foot of the bed. I smiled and greeted him openly without fear. Otto floated over to the side of the bed and stopped near my pillow. I stared at Otto with wonderment. I couldn't help but notice the luminescent brilliance of my spiritual friend. The warm angelical glow that emanated from him was awe inspiring. Then, abruptly and without warning, I received mental information that completely obliterated the last few remnants of my religious upbringing.

I want to share what I now believe to be an unescapable self-realization. My guide, my guardian angel, my Otto-matic pilot, I believe is my _Higher Self_. It stretches far beyond my imagination to fabricate a concept like this one. But I believe the being is me, in a higher form of consciousness. An inner part of me somehow understood that this "Oversoul" as Jane Roberts referred to it, has been with me from my physical beginning. In essence, he has always been with me, and always will be. I am he, and the I that is he, is me.

Abruptly and inadvertently I reconnected; Kathy moved again. I moved physically away from her and attempted to return to the paralysis to no avail. Moving physically had somehow disrupted the continuity of the OBE. I lay there completely connected and awake.

★ RETROSPECT

I am at a retrospective loss, yet thousands of thoughts race through my mind colliding with one another. An ever present realization has permanently merged with my beliefs. I now know that I am not alone, I will not be alone, nor have I ever been alone! I believe that I am guided by my Higher Self, which in turn is guided by "All That Is" (my name for God).

At a recent IANDS meeting, a newcomer, sharing her experience for the first time, spoke of an expression that her angel/guide said to her which left her puzzled. Toward the end of her NDE, just before she returned to her body, her spiritual guide shared this insight: "The smaller light follows the larger, and the larger light follows the *Source*." To me, the meaning of this statement was very apparent and significant.

❧   ❧   ❧

7 November 1994, (Meditated prior to pre-flight)

I fell asleep early, about 9:00 p.m., and woke at 1:00. I tossed and turned until 3:30 (the interrupted sleep technique, sort of!). I lay there mentally reaching out for the paralysis. It slowly crept over me like a river of warm honey. I focused on picking a destination and casually thought of walking in our den. I ceased to be in my body in our bedroom and materialized in the den.

I paused and asked myself, "Am I dreaming?" The blinking out at one location and blinking in at another threw me off guard. I panned the room as I started to walk through the house. I floated up about five inches and skipped through one of the bedrooms to my four-year-old son's bedroom door. I paused, walked through the door, and slid over to Devon's bed. I noticed that he had kicked off the blankets I so carefully had tucked in. I began to hover over his bed, feeling very protective of this frail little being. I was his daddy, his astral security guard.

I left my son's bedroom through the wall, performed a quick patrol of the rest of the house, then casually thought of my body. As if I were on an invisible conveyor belt, I headed toward my bedroom. Reconnection was so slightly noticeable I wasn't sure if it had happened or not. The little finger trick placed me back at the helm.

★ RETROSPECT

I find the seemingly endless variables simply amazing. I seem to be able to fly to a location or "blink out" and "blink in" to wherever my thoughts are focused. Incredible!

What are we that we can do these wondrous things?

I have found that during an OBE, emotions seem to be greatly intensified, almost as if I become the emotion itself. I have also found that the "love emotion" appears to be much stronger. For example, the feeling of love for my son was greatly intensified as I hovered over his bed.

❧　　❧　　❧

11 November 1994 (Nothing out of the ordinary)

I laid down not thinking of attempting an OBE, although any and all were welcome.

☾ OBE BEGINS

I became aware of the paralysis but was not fully focused on the feeling of falling backwards or the shortness of breath that sometimes accompanies it. Before I could file my mental flight plan, I winked out of my physical body with no destination in mind. I knew immediately that I was not at the controls, and that something was amiss.

I winked into the middle of nowhere. All around me there was an endless darkness; except directly in front of me, there was a single source bright light. It was as if a blue-white star burned a hole in the middle of a black velvet curtain.

The "Light" radiated outward in long bright shards, like a crystal comprised of thousands of needle-like spears. The shards penetrated my very soul. I can best describe this whole experience from the perspective of the reentry heat shield on the Apollo 11 space capsule.

As the space capsule's heat shield resisted the extreme temperatures of an earth reentry, microscopic pieces were vaporized and burned away. The Light pierced through me. Like the capsule's heat shield, parts of *me* were burned away. Parts I no longer needed. The Light was excruciatingly wonderful. I was wrenched from the Light and tossed back into my body.

"Are you okay?" Kathy asked.

"I'm all right," I said wondering why I came back so abruptly.

"You were moaning, so I shook you," Kathy explained.

At this point, I tried not to focus on my swift return because I wanted desperately to go back.

Ꙭ OBE CONTINUES

I didn't have long to wait. I felt the paralysis and winked out. I winked into the same locale as before, and there was the radiant brilliance. And just as before, I felt the unwanted pieces of myself being burned away.

Consciously this entire scene was alien to me, but subconsciously this whole series of events was completely familiar and welcome.

"Oh, what a heavenly light!"

Then, without warning, I was slammed back into my body, *hard*!

"Are you all right?" Kathy asked.

"Yes, I'm fine!" I responded feeling a little irritated. I refrained from showing it because I'd learned my lesson from a previous mistake. Try as I might, I was not able to return to the Light. The feeling of irritation severed the OBE chain of events.

★ RETROSPECT

Note to the would be traveler: The feeling of anger is extremely pernicious to the chain of events which lead to an OBE. Any and all negative emotions will likely stifle any attempts you make to achieve a higher state of consciousness.

❧   ❧   ❧

17 November 1994 (Tired, very sleepy)

I could barely stay awake. I read for a while then fell asleep for the night, or so I thought! Kathy woke at 1:30, got up to check on our son Devon, then got back into bed with a thump!

I was now awake. I lay there feeling completely abandoned by the Sandman. I tossed and turned until 3:20 a.m.—on a week night! The thought of driving to work semi-comatose did not appeal to me.

"Well Al, since you've practically performed the interrupted sleep technique, you may as well top it off with a pre-flight!" I thought to myself.

"Okay, I will!" I was ready to try anything at that point. I completed the pre-flight, disengaged my astral parking brake, and waited. After about ten minutes, I could feel the paralysis creeping up from behind. I greeted the paralysis with open arms and released the physical.

☾ OBE BEGINS

My ears were assaulted by a loud crackling. I focused my thoughts, heard a loud "pop," and was literally tossed out of my body.

As if I were being summoned, I headed straight for the wall that separated the living room from our bedroom. Without hesitation I dove through the wall and quickly came to an abrupt halt. I had emerged partially into a black empty void. The upper half of my astral self was in the void, and the lower half was still in my bedroom. "Another new variable," I thought. I increased the sensitivity of all my astral radar.

There was no sound, surface, or light source to follow; just a nothingness that seemed to stretch in all directions. Although I could not see it, I sensed a barrier of some kind far, far ahead of me.

I released my parking brake, and like a car going down a steep hill, I moved forward, with gradually increasing speed. After what seemed like an eternity, I slammed on the brake and screeched to a halt. "Turn around before you get lost," my fear commanded.

I looked for a landmark, or should I say a "void-mark," but the darkness was endless. I thought, "What if there's nothing on the other side?"

After checking to see if I'd changed my orientation or attitudinal position, I mentally put myself into reverse and backed out the way I came in—feet first. I felt a surface behind me and backed right through it to my bedroom.

"Maybe you should try this direction some other time!" I turned toward the bedroom door and floated into the hallway. I floated down to the carpet and walked into the living room to examine the wall I should have emerged from earlier. There was nothing peculiar about the wall on this side. I decided to perform a quick reconnaissance of the house.

I zipped through the kitchen and into the den. Observing nothing out of the ordinary, I turned and retraced my path. I turned the corner and headed toward the living room and almost ran right into Otto. I ceased moving. From this point on I will offer the remainder of the excursion as a retrospect, because the memory of it occurred later that morning.

★ RETROSPECT:

I remember returning to my body, and as I opened my eyes I paused, feeling the memory of this OBE slip from my grasp. I rose from the bed struggling with the images dancing in my head. Was I out of body, or not? Why can't I recall what happened? I remember leaving my body then. . . I was in the den . . . no, I was in the living room and . . . what is going on?

I showered, got dressed, and left for work. I sat at my desk for a short while, got up and walked to the restroom. I stood there staring at my reflection in the mirror when the veil of forgetfulness was abruptly snatched away. "Oh my God, I remember!"

★ RETROSPECTIVE OBE CONTINUES

As I screeched to a halt, after rounding the corner from the kitchen, Otto was waiting for me. Another entity stood a few feet away but did not approach us. No words were exchanged just images and feelings. And all of this seemed very familiar to me. It was as if I have been interfacing with the two of them, in this manner, for a very long time.

I sensed that the entity a few feet away was not here because of me but because of my wife Kathy. Could this be her guide or angel? What also occurred to me was that I felt no fear, at all! I felt myself being recalled to my body. Without resisting, I quickly returned to the physical.

★ RETROPSECT ON RETROSPECT

I can't help but wonder if Franklin D. Roosevelt knew when he said, "You have nothing to fear but fear itself," that this applied to the soul traveler as well.

I began to wonder about my memory loss, and the difficulty I had in recalling the OBE encounter. Was I *not* supposed to remember the encounter with the other entity? And if so why? Normally, I have no problem recalling my experiences, but this time it was extremely arduous.

I wonder how many times a spirit has communicated with my soul unbeknownst to my personality self. Is this how these beings guide and direct us during the course of our lives? And is this guidance normally on a subconscious level? I can't help but think about the many times that I've suddenly remembered a dream that was somehow suppressed or forgotten. Could this be one of the hurdles we must leap if we are to truly progress spiritually? Must we somehow become consciously aware of this spiritual communication as it transpires?

10

PLANES OF CONSCIOUSNES

> "We fear the darkness only because we don't know what is there."
> —**Robert Monroe**

In this chapter I'd like to share with the reader and future soul traveler a little information on what it is like to explore the multiple levels of consciousness, primarily the astral plane. As you may know, access to this information has been shrouded with secrecy since the beginning of time. I believe one reason for the mystique is the foreboding category in which it has been placed—primarily the occult.

The levels of consciousness as explained by Eckankar are: the physical, astral, causal, mental, and etheric planes. Information about these levels has been distorted by countless dogmatic teachings.

It appears that a vast majority of people are afraid to learn more about the occult because of fearful condemnations like, "It is the work of the Devil!" In other cases some individuals have been literally denied access to this ancient wisdom because they were deemed spiritually unqualified. In the past, knowledge of this sort could only be acquired by dedicating months or years of study in remotely isolated ashrams and/or monasteries.

An ashram is a religious retreat for a colony of disciples, usually headed by one or more persons who have dedicated their lives to spiritual evolution of the soul. These individuals are usually referred to as masters.

For those future soul travelers it is important to acquire as much knowledge as possible, preferably before one sets sail into the world of what I like to call the "dearly, but not departed."

It is my aim to share some of this knowledge with the reader—hoping this will assist you in avoiding detours or road blocks that will surely be encountered.

I find it extremely disheartening that due to fearful religious dogmas, the western culture has been left behind in the quest for spiritual enlightenment. Hindus and Buddhists of eastern civilizations appear to be further along the path of spiritual advancement. The religions of the east readily accept their spiritual origins and destiny and continue to seek further spiritual guidance and awareness. The concept of reincarnation, for example, is not only accepted but encouraged and taught. However, in the modern western society, this concept is assuredly in the embryonic stages of development. In spite of the widely accepted teachings of Edgar Cayce and the profound insights given by the entity Seth via Jane Roberts, this awareness remains obscure and virtually unexplored.

In these writings it is my intention to provide some reassurance for those who are fearful and provide a partial road map for the more adventurous. You need not be fearful when delving into the many levels of consciousness, because it is a *natural* part of our existence.

As you have learned earlier, it has not been an easy struggle for me to overcome my own unfounded fears. Deep within myself, I have found my fear to come from or be driven by a basic "fight or flee" survival instinct. As you probably know, without this survival instinct, we would not have endured the many hazards this earth life system has placed before us.

More likely we would have gone the way of the dinosaur and become extinct. If early man had not run screaming into his subterranean shelters or massed together to repel a ravenous predator, we would not have survived.

This basic survival instinct, however, is not a

prerequisite for exploring the astral plane and beyond; nor is it needed. And for myself it has been more of a hindrance than an asset.

One of the first things to understand about the astral plane is that it is not devoid of life. The beings there will be quite unlike anything you may be familiar with. But don't kid yourself; they are very real. Be advised that the level of spiritual enlightenment achieved by these beings may vary a great deal. In addition, just because the life forms there qualify as spirits and will likely possess far greater capabilities than most of us, it does not mean that all are wise and forthright.

When a person has passed on to a higher level of consciousness, that person doesn't automatically become an angel, guide, or spirit master. I have found that we retain a great many characteristics composed of who we are in this life, both the positive and the negative.

This does not mean that these entities should be feared; it just means that not all encounters with them will necessarily be for your higher good. The astral plane, as you may know by now, is just one place we go when our bodies die. However you end up there, be it death or soul travel, you may experience a variety of unexplainable sounds. The Eckist refer to these sounds as the voice of Sugmad or God.

I myself have heard many different sounds during soul travel. Strangely enough, many of these sounds were listed on a rather intricate chart given to me by the Eckist.

For instance, the sound associated with the astral plane is the roaring of the sea. The causal plane is the tinkling of bells. The mental plane is running water, and the etheric is buzzing bees. (Does this sound familiar?) The focus of this chapter will remain on the astral plane.

The astral plane may seem like a place to go; but in actuality it is something you become aware of. The astral plane, like oxygen, permeates the physical plane. On the astral plane we unconsciously create a "body double" comprised of astral material. This astral body, like the physical body, serves as a containment vehicle for the soul.

As I have mentioned earlier, it provides transitional stability for the newly dead as well as the soul traveler. Nevertheless, it is not permanent nor is it absolutely needed. I have slipped out of it, leaving it behind like a worn out pair of coveralls. If you manage to accomplish this, you will still retain all the simulated senses you have in the physical: sight, sound, touch, and in rare situations taste.

The power of thought is a tool during the out of body experience that must be handled carefully and clearly. Remember, anything you can imagine you will see or experience. This alone may indicate the awesome capabilities of our soul.

I have come to believe that thought is just as powerful in the physical as in the astral or beyond. After all, everything around you presently began as a thought in someone's mind, it just didn't manifest instantly as it would have on the astral plane.

Now, there are many avenues to take while touring the astral plane; but all the while be advised that deceased loved ones and strangers may present themselves with little or no warning.

In the beginning keep your jaunts localized, gradually venturing further as you gain more confidence. Remember, physical locations on this planet and beyond are merely a thought away. You can quickly get in over your head in the wink of an eye, so keep it short and simple.

Future or past life events may also be presented to the soul traveler. This I have not yet experienced. I've also been told that spiritual healing of loved ones or your own body is possible.

In early 1992, I was diagnosed with the debilitating disease of multiple sclerosis, better known as MS. After suffering two devastating attacks, I was hospitalized with severe vision and equilibrium problems. My prognosis was not good. My doctor explained to me that my physical health would likely degrade over the next few years. Shortly after receiving this less than welcome news, I began to have consciously controlled OBEs. I knew at that time that I had very little to loose by trying this method of healing. Well to make a long story short, be it coincidence or not, I can gratefully state that I have absolutely *no* outward symptoms or physical manifestations of this otherwise crippling disease. This appears to be one more puzzle in a series of puzzles that I have experienced.

NDE'ers, as they are sometimes called, have shared OBEs with me involving a great hall of records.

The Akashic records are alleged to be everything a soul has experienced in its many reincarnational lives, including karmic lessons. Karmic lessons are structured to help and sometimes force the stubborn soul to progress spiritually. To date, I have not seen or read these records in my travels, but it is on my "things to do" list.

The subject of religious dogmas is important. But first, I must clarify that it is not for me to say what a person should or should not believe. We, as beings of light, have a "free will," and it is because of this freedom to choose that the soul is capable of spiritual progression.

For you would-be soul travelers, there may exist within you certain religious dogmas that will prevent you from transcending the astral. Believe it or not, there are some religious beliefs that do not exist above the astral plane. When you become aware of these dogmas, you will be able to experience the multiple dimensions above the astral plane. I have had to discard and continue to discard, no matter how painful, antiquated beliefs to which I held dear. You may find this painfully necessary when searching for your own ultimate truth.

I once read a book a friend recommended called *Ask your Angels*. The basic premise is angels have wings. It also states that everyone has his/her own invisible wings.

I wonder if this is a way of providing something for humans to relate to by merging tangible wings with unbelievable creatures such as angels. Does this make them easier to accept? The only concern I have with a prejudgment of this sort is this: a person who is unfamiliar with the creative magic that is always present on the astral plane, may impose his own visual images onto another being. This will likely contaminate the OBE and prevent the traveler from having a dogma-free experience.

I won't pretend that I have seen every type of nonphysical entity that may exist (thank God!), but none that I saw had wings. *I* fly without wings. I would think that the angels do too! In comparison, I am in my first day of preschool, and the Angels are Ph.D's.

11 January 95, 10:30 P.M. (Taylor pre-flight)

After performing a pre-flight, I released and . . . fell asleep. I woke up about 1:00 A.M. feeling a slight bit of the vibes. I performed another pre-flight and slipped into the paralysis as if it were a custom-made suit.

☾ OBE BEGINS

Soon with the help of my astral vision, I began to slowly scan the bedroom. Unexpectedly, outside the window I heard my dog, a German Shepherd named Bear, barking frantically. Normally Bear sleeps inside the house at night, but evidently one of us forgot to let him in. Why was he barking right outside my bedroom window? In the seven years we've had him, he has never done that. I reconnected with my body and sat up. Bear immediately stopped barking. I curiously parted the curtain and looked out of the window. I could see Bear calmly walking back from the other side of the backyard. I got out of bed, let him in, and went back to bed, grounded for the rest of the night.

★ RETROSPECT

Did Bear somehow know I was out of body? He stopped barking the moment I reconnected as if he knew, and started walking away from the window even before I looked out. Are animals sensitive to astral forms or the disembodied life force? Did Bear sense some type of energy field I was generating? This may be worth investigating later.

❧　　　❧　　　❧

14 January 95, 2:00 A.M. (Taylor pre-flight)

For some reason I had trouble falling asleep and tossed and turned until shortly after midnight. Finally something started to happen, even though sleep was initially my goal.

☾ OBE BEGINS:

The presence of the paralysis was heralded by a swarm of buzzing bees. Astrally I sprang to the sitting position and looked casually around the bedroom. I focused on floating and rose a foot or so above the blankets. I became aware of the sound of water coming from the other side of the bedroom door. I began to recognize the splashing sound; it was the shower in the bathroom.

I wondered why Kathy decided to take a shower in the middle of the night. As I focused on the sound, the door and wall, which separated our bedroom from the hallway, abruptly ceased to be a visual obstacle. I could see the bathroom door framed by the light within, which was physically impossible.

My attention shifted slightly, and I became aware of a humanoid figure lying in the bed next to my body. Oh my God! If Kathy is in the bathroom taking a shower, then what was this resting beside me?

I began probing the figure with a part of my consciousness. I was amazed at what transpired because I was not using my astral hands to identify this reclining intruder, I was using pure thought. I could mentally touch this being from head to toe all at the same time.

Who is this? Fear crept over me. I bolted toward my body using the abort sequence, the little finger trick, and fright. I reconnected at the same moment I felt a familiar elbow.

"Are you okay?" Kathy asked.

"Uh, yes . . . I'm fine." I replied realizing the blatant error in observation I had just made. Kathy was not taking a shower, my older son was. Feeling a tad foolish, I was lying down now listening to the sounds of Brandon completing his shower and turning off the water.

★ RETROSPECT

The next morning I asked Brandon why he had decided to take a shower at two o'clock in the morning. "Dad, I didn't get off work until 1:30 this morning," he said. "Sorry, did I wake you up?"

"No, I was already awake, sort of."

Soul Traveler

11

BEAUTIFUL DREAMER

> *"Dreams are the language of the soul, and because we dream every night, it is important we learn this language!"*
> **—Ruth Montgomery**

Have you ever asked yourself or wondered why we dream? Everybody does it, but why? One third of our lives is spent lying on our backs. During this state of seeming inactivity, the mind is actively at work. Some people believe that dreams are messages from the subconscious giving us clues to solve our everyday problems. Others believe there is very little value in these late night fantasies. I too believe dreams are clues to daily existence, but this is just the tip of the iceberg.

Why is it that during the dream state people have reported a variety of incidents which seem to link this state of consciousness with the physical world? A woman once told me she had misplaced her car keys and was unable to locate them for several days. One night, after searching frantically for them, she gave up and went to bed. After lying down for the night, she once again thought of her misplaced keys and prayed for assistance before drifting off to sleep. Sometime during the night it came to her in a dream that her keys were resting inside of a multi-colored vase. Upon waking the next morning she remembered the dream and recalled having a similar vase in her living room. Leaping from the bed and charging into the living room, she grabbed the vase and poured out its contents. There to her surprise were her missing keys just as the dream had foretold.

If we were to scan the distant and not so distant past, we would find numerous tales similar to this one. The Bible, for example, is riddled with tales of people's dreams where they are given insight and solutions to problems. I believe, however these types of events are not restricted to an individual's beliefs or lack there of. In fact, these types of occurrences have transcended religion and have influenced the atheist as well.

So, what is going on? During my many experiments with altered states of consciousness, I have experienced a "knowing" that has been accessible upon leaving the body.

However, I do not believe that one must travel outside of the body to tap into this energy source. This seemingly infinite source of energy has been described as a "universal consciousness" by prominent researchers like Dr. Joseph Murphy.

This universal consciousness, I believe, is the same energy source that psychics and mediums somehow tap into. Residing in this extreme level of consciousness is an inexhaustible amount of information.

Depending on an individual's perceptions, accessed information will manifest itself in symbols, images, feelings, and sometimes in an unexplainable "knowing." In other cases the receiver of the data may not be adept at interpreting this information and he may require the assistance of a spiritual guide. If there is a significant desire or need for information, the guide may act as a conduit and convey this data to the receiver. However, I do not believe information extricated from this universal consciousness flows completely unrestricted, depending on the individuals karmic requirements. I also do not believe our futures are predetermined or predestined.

And based on this premise, I believe our futures are only probable. In other words, our "probable futures" are what *might* happen as opposed to what *will* happen. And depending on the soul's spiritual needs, data received via the universal consciousness will either be denied or severely restricted. It may be that a superior wisdom has imposed unalterable "safeguards" or data flow limitations which appears to work in *our own best interest*. The amount of data we can access may be governed by the impact it will have on the totality of our earth life experience.

Now, a few words about one of the more exciting types of nocturnal imaging, the *lucid* dream. Lucid dreams are defined as: "The state or quality of being aware that one is dreaming. Bright with the radiance of intellect; not darkened or confused; clear and distinct awareness."

In childhood and as a young adult I would literally "wake up in my dreams." In the past this is how I described the feeling of being alert and aware after having become extremely lucid. I would then fend off any monsters or creatures that had the misfortune of crossing my path.

Sometimes a nightmare would become so horrific it would force me to ask myself, "Is this a dream?" After which my mind would literally wake up while my body remained asleep. I was then capable of changing the script and the plot of the dream. In short, I became an actor and director. When you stop accepting the role of a hapless passenger, you can literally seize the helm and steer a course toward calmer sea if you want to. In my case, if that meant I had to assume the identity of Superman, then so be it. All in all there seemed to be very little I could not do as long as my thoughts remained focused.

The key to becoming lucid during a dream begins while you are still awake. While you are out going about your daily routines, periodically ask yourself, "Am I dreaming?" Practicing this exercise while awake may condition you to question your state of consciousness while dreaming. It works for me!

Soul Traveler

12

THE ULTIMATE TRUTH

> *"Before I formed thee in the belly, I knew thee; and before thou camest forth out of the womb, I sanctified thee..."*
> **—Jeremiah (1:5):**

So, what is the ultimate truth? Well, before we delve into this mystery of mysteries, perhaps we should first ask the ultimate question. For me that question is: why are we here? I will not pretend that I have found this elusive pot of gold, but I will offer a viewpoint highly influenced by my soul travels. There are several "known" elements that I will use to support my opinions and conjectures. It is from this perspective that I will probe the verity behind the earth life experience.

The first known element is that we exist independently of our physical bodies, hence the ability to travel out of the body. For me this has been proof enough that I will survive death's embrace. Secondly, we must accept that a multitude of beings exist in a dimension other than the physical. Thirdly, it has been well documented that during hypnosis and after an NDE, hundreds of people have reported experiencing a detailed review of their lives. How many times have we heard the expression, "My life literally flashed before my eyes!" This phrase has always been associated with life threatening circumstances. At this point I must query why would a review of past indiscretions be of some value after departing from the world of the living? If we die and go to heaven, hell or somewhere in between, of what possible benefit is a review of what is now unchangeable? Could it be we are given this life review in order to learn by our mistakes, in hopes of not repeating them? I suggest that this may be one of our first clues that we somehow return to the earth life system. And if so, then what is to be gained by returning to experience another life? Could it be to facilitate spiritual evolution of the soul?

I have personally come to believe that life without reincarnation is like a stage play with only one act. There just isn't enough time for character development.

So, providing we do somehow return to the physical and live again, where will all these life lessons eventually lead us? Is there some distant yet attainable goal? Based on my spiritual travels, I would say YES, beyond a shadow of a doubt!

On the physical plane you are born, grow up, grow older, and finally experience death. It is then that some NDE'ers report being drawn into a tunnel filled with swirling multi-colored lights. Some report no lights at all, just an eerie blackness (which sounds similar to the black void I've experienced). When they arrive at the end of this tunnel, numerous NDE'ers recall being met by a deceased relative or one or more beings of light. This generally occurs on the astral plane. According to the *Tibetan Book of the Dead* this location or state of consciousness is referred to as the "bardo."

This appears to be a good time to issue my first and only word of warning to the would-be soul traveler. As I have mentioned earlier, on April 3, 1993 during an early morning OBE, I experienced an overwhelming feeling of finally coming home. And only after a myriad of repeat visits have I come to accept this state of consciousness as the bardo. Since then, I continue to have a deep longing for what I now know to be home. This longing has become a permanent part of my waking consciousness. I am constantly homesick! So be advised, you too may develop this agonizing longing for home.

Sometime after exiting the tunnel, it is then that a life review must be endured. I say endured because looking back at one's own life has been described as a mixture of pleasure and devastating sadness. The extent of sadness usually depends on how kind or cruel a person has been to others. NDE'ers have described feeling the exact same pain, sadness, and hurt they thoughtlessly and selfishly caused another.

After the life review, a soul now has the opportunity to plan the next step on its own evolutionary path.

Using a chart depicting the various arcs of spiritual evolution, I will share with the reader additional pieces to this puzzle. There are probably a multitude of evolutionary paths an individual soul may follow or choose; but for the sake of simplicity, I have limited this illustration to these five paths.

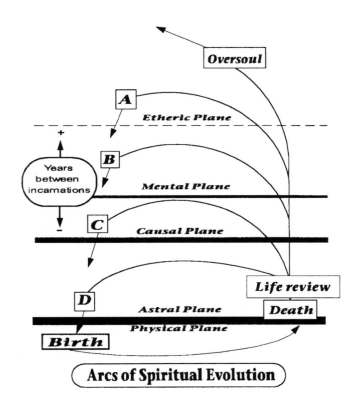

Arcs of Spiritual Evolution

On the arc chart the "D" arc represents a type of soul often referred to as earthbound. This type of soul has also been affectionately nicknamed a "repeater." This is because the type "D" must reincarnate numerous times to gain a minimal amount of enlightenment. These souls ignore essential insights given during the life review and often fail to satisfy inescapable karmic requirements.

Without the necessary planning, the "D" type of soul is likely to quickly reincarnate missing the opportunistic benefits of careful planning. The type "D" soul has also been blamed for a vast amount of the world's heartache and sorrows. This type of soul is usually narcissistic and self destructive.

Arcs "C" and "B" depict a soul at a higher state of evolution. This type of soul is deeply affected by the life review and usually is deeply remorseful when confronted with their past transgressions. These souls will generally direct more energy towards preparation and planning for the next life. At the "C" and "B" stages of evolution, the time spent in the bardo will increase allowing for higher arcs into the upper levels of consciousness. These souls are just becoming aware of who and what they truly are.

The type "A" soul is a highly developed being and has attained a very high level of self awareness during its physical incarnation. While living on the physical plane, these souls are usually spiritual teachers, masters, or shamans. The type "A" soul often has a profound impact on the human population as a whole. These enlightened souls may very well be messengers from God. Some of them have been labeled a Saint, a master, a guide and or prophet. The primary focus of this type of entity is to lead lost souls back to All That Is (God).

Last, but not least, is the Oversoul entity, a being of unimaginable capabilities and possibilities. This type of self-aware consciousness is virtually unlimited. This being is no longer tied to the seemingly endless cycle of reincarnation. The Oversoul entity has been referred to as a god in the making. An Oversoul is a being that has progressed light years from the "A" type soul. In truth there is very little comparison. The Oversoul is rapidly progressing toward the ultimate truth, which is to become a co-worker and co-creator with God. I believe this is the irrevocable destiny of the soul. This brings to mind the expression, "We are *all* created in God's own image." After slipping free of my astral body and existing as a pin point of consciousness, being created in God's own image continues to possess possibilities far beyond these earthly vehicles of flesh and bone.

13

PRE-FLIGHT PREPARATIONS

> *"When we realize our thoughts create our future experiences, then looking within ourselves for happiness becomes our only recourse."*
> **—Soul Traveler**

If you have read this far, then you must be asking yourself, "How can I do that?" When I inquired as to what percentage of people who actually achieved a controlled conscious OBE, I was told about twenty to thirty-five percent. I'm not trying to discourage anyone. I just want to suggest that a trial of patience may be in store for you.

These techniques are not guaranteed, of course. They are just some examples of what I've tried with a certain amount of success. Try them all until you feel comfortable or achieve some results. If you fall asleep, don't be concerned; because you may be closer than you think.

If you feel more comfortable surrounding yourself with white light, then do so. If you like to use crystals, then use them. The goal here is to get as relaxed as possible. If these items help you to accomplish this, that's all that matters. One other thing you must remember, prior to traveling and during soul travel, is that you are a being of light and nothing can harm you unless you think it can. Even then, after the experience, you will emerge unblemished.

The spiritual path that I have taken has sometimes been a bumpy one, but I now know that every emotional twist and turn has brought me to this point. I have found that emotions like stress, anger, envy or negative thoughts hamper if not sever the chain of events leading up to an OBE. So, get rid of them. (Piece of cake, right?) It is important to approach this type of experience with as much inner peace as possible. This is something that can't be faked, you must be steadfast in achieving this state.

Anger, hate, and envy will point you in the opposite direction of inner peace.

I have found after careful examination of the "big picture" in the majority of contentious situations, the outcome had very little long-term negative impact on my life. But the associated tension has had a profound impact, no OBEs!

I have switched to acquiescing in personal disputes, rather than holding stubbornly to my own point of view. Sometimes we defend our correctness to the brink of insanity. Remember, inner peace is the goal, and that peace should reflect in as many areas of your life as possible.

I don't believe that stress, tension, or any other emotion can be extinguished by merely throwing a mental switch. The effects or remnants of negative emotions may require thorough housekeeping deep within even though there are few visible indications on the surface. This negativity may be at work on a subconscious level preventing you from achieving total relaxation. In other words, you won't be going anywhere!

I often wonder why we must prove we are right, and someone else wrong?

Why must there always be a superior and a subordinate?

Why must we constantly jockey for a position of authority?

Why must we strive to establish a pecking order, when none is needed?

Why must we be one up or one down?

I am not suggesting that in situations where you may have concerns for your own or someone's safety you should not stick to your convictions. However, when the stress of being incorrect is far less than the stress of proving correctness, why choose the latter—especially if neither outcome has a long term affect on your life?

One more reason why we shouldn't hold such inflexible views is that we don't all think the same way.

It frequently appears as if we all create and operate in simultaneous yet slightly different realities. For instance, two people can be exposed to the same situation yet perceive and recall the event differently.

My wife and I were strolling through the aisles of the local supermarket, when I experienced one of these "slightly different realities." Shuffling past the dairy section I noticed a plastic bottle with pink liquid in it. It reminded me of the strawberry drink I enjoyed as a kid. I began to scan the label when Kathy walked over to where I was standing. Taking the bottle and looking at the label she said, "This stuff is full of calories. You really should read the label."

With a puzzled look I replied, "That's exactly what I was doing when you took the bottle!"

"You handed the bottle to me!" Kathy defended.

After reviewing a mental recording of the last minute or two, I launched back at her, "No I didn't!"

"Yes you did!" Kathy said showing signs of irritation. I was amazed at the clear and unyielding differences we had on what had just transpired. I then realized that this "slightly different reality" could easily escalate to full blown verbal hostilities. I called a truce and reflected on our differences. So, let someone be right, or wrong, or just let that person BE! Remember, he or she may be just as confident in their particular point of view!

My personal rules for life are simply stated by this basic credo which helps me to balance my existence, in the body, and *out*.

Judge, and you shall be judged.
Hate, and you shall be hated.
Lie, and you shall be lied to.
Cheat, and you shall be cheated.
Curse, and you shall be cursed,
but Love, and so shall you be.

If all people would adhere to this simple yet challenging guidance, no doubt we'd all be charting a steady course toward spiritual enlightenment. I believe that whatever you put into your experiences is ultimately what you'll get out of them.

There appears to be two dominant emotions we take with us when we leave this world, love and fear. The latter of which pushes us further away from All That Is, and the former speaks for itself. God and love are synonymous. Remember, how we relate to one another has a profound physical and spiritual impact on all of us as a whole. And I believe we will ultimately have to account for this.

Soul Traveler

14

THE VOYAGE HOME

"Fear is for people who don't know God!"

The thoughts we think on a daily basis are all too often generated by the things we fear! For example, fear of being alone, penniless, homeless, jobless, and loveless, just to name a few. These fears have a profound effect on the actions and decisions each of us must choose in the course of our every day lives. It is because of these fears that we either spring into action when none is needed, or fail to take action when we know we should.

We seem to constantly be afraid of what MIGHT happen! And as you know, what might happen is always bad. We then allow our behaviors to be controlled by this fear instead of being lead by our higher selves. Ironically, it is because of this fear the vast majority of us haven't the slightest clue that there is a higher self. Thus, fear becomes an impenetrable curtain between the personality self and the God within. So, simply put, fear is for people who don't know God! If you arrive at this realization you will have very little difficulty during your own soul travels.

In conclusion I offer the following techniques and mental exercises in hoping they will serve you as they have me.

The Paralysis State

It is important to find a warm, not hot, quiet, cozy, safe place to perform any of the following exercises. Once you have started, do not move under any circumstance—not even to scratch your nose! Don't move!

I'd like to address in more detail the sensations before, during, and after the paralysis. Based on my earlier writings and inquiries, there is a good chance that some readers may be currently experiencing some sort of night paralysis. I want to discuss some specifics that they alone may relate to.

As the paralysis begins to creep over you, a feeling of falling backwards may accompany it. This sensation may cause you to react by catching or stopping yourself. If you react in this manner it might break the chain of events and abort your disconnection from the physical. You may also feel like you cannot breathe properly, but this will quickly pass. If you get through to this point you may become aware of a variety of sounds at a deafening volume—sounds such as buzzing, roaring wind, electrical sizzling, crackling, and even a musical tone or instrument. At this point do not guess, imagine, or attempt to identify the sounds at all. You will be at that mysterious place where dreams are born. Keep your thoughts clear or you might be confronted by your own creation, two heads and all!

Later, as you develop more control you may want to experiment by creating a dream to experience. This will likely take a lot of practice. If you transition this stage you may hear *voices* or see *shapes* and *images*. Having circumvented these distractions you may also become aware of a floating or upward movement. This sometimes occurs without asking. If you are not rising skyward, try repeating the command to do so; this may work. Remember there is nothing to fear but your own fearful uncontrolled imagination, and also you cannot be injured or killed. However, be advised you can feel pain if you believe you have been injured by something or someone. In addition, you need not worry about returning to your body, because the slightest thought of this will make it so. You also do not have to worry about someone taking over control of your body. Divine Power has given it to you, and you alone. So let go and enjoy!

Full Relaxation Routine

Lie flat on your back with your arms at your sides and close your eyes. This is called the earth position. Make sure that your head is supported naturally, not propped up with extra pillows; one is usually sufficient. Starting at your feet, tighten the muscles in your toes and feet. Hold for ten to fifteen seconds then allow the tension to melt down into the mattress or floor. Repeat this for your other leg muscles, your ankles, calves, thighs, etc. Continue this process until you reach your face, but don't forget your neck and shoulder muscles. Tighten and relax your jaw, cheeks, and forehead. Now tighten your hands into a clenched fist and hold it. Slowly begin to tighten the forearm and upper arm (biceps and triceps). When you've done this, hold your entire arm rigid for approximately twenty seconds. Release, and allow all the tension to melt away. Slowly scan your body, mentally looking for any tension that you may have missed. If necessary, repeat the tighten and release procedure.

Now lie there breathing normally and repeat in your mind, "I want to float upward." Try to be patient. It may take a lot of practice, and in the beginning you may just drift off to sleep. Try not to become frustrated or tense, you will just be defeating yourself. So relax!

The Taylor Pre-flight

Lie flat on your back in the earth position. Take in a deep breath and hold for approximately four seconds; then release the breath through slightly parted lips, as you sing the Hu. Try using a low vibrating tone while you exhale slowly. You may need to first practice the Hu to find a tone level you feel comfortable with. If you are worried about disturbing your mate, you can Hu, just softly.

Mentally begin relaxing your muscles, starting at your feet. Move through each set of muscles similar to the full relaxation routine; but relax them only. Do not tighten your muscles this time. Breathe normally and think about floating or rising upwards. Remember, be patient.

Abbreviated Pre-flight

Assume the earth position, close your eyes and get comfortable. Imagine a three foot diameter ball of warm glowing energy suspended two feet above you. Breathe in deeply and rhythmically, but not forcefully. As you inhale, mentally pull a stream of energy down from the ball. Go down and through the bottom of your feet up into your lungs. When you exhale, push the energy up and out the top of your head, back into the ball of energy above you. As the energy enters your feet and legs, feel the relaxing warmth it brings. Let this warmth flow through your entire body as you become part of the energy circle. Mentally release control of your arms and legs, they are no longer a part of you. Relax and listen for an inner signal. (Buzzing, crackling, zipping, roaring wind or sparks of light.) Again, be patient. You may just fall asleep. (Note: At this point I have been able to start the vibes or slip into the paralysis.)

Pre-programming

This technique may seem easy but sometimes the simplest things work the best. Go to bed as you normally do. Then repeat aloud, "I want to have an out of body!" Or spell aloud several times the phrase astral travel, A-S-T-R-A-L T-R-A-V-E-L. Pronounce every letter two or three times, then let go of all your thoughts (easier said than done). Repeat this three or four times if you need to do so.

Interrupted Sleep Technique (IST)

This exercise can be used alone or combined with any of the other techniques. As I have described earlier in this book, go to sleep about 9:00 P.M., set the alarm for 1:00 A.M. Get out of bed. It will not be effective if you wake up then go right back to sleep, so get out of bed! Stay up until 3:30 A.M., lay flat on your back, and relax. I usually chant the Hu or use a breathing technique that is similar.

Focus on an Object

This routine is very difficult to master. The first few times I tried it, I ended up falling asleep. Lie down and perform a breathing routine that suits you. Ten minutes is usually sufficient. Stay flat on your back and relax. In your mind's eye picture a simple object like a square or triangle. Remember to keep it simple, a square or triangle will be difficult enough to focus on without your thoughts drifting off somewhere. If your thoughts do drift away from your primary focus, gently bring them back to your chosen image. You will quickly find out that the mind loves to wander. You will also find out that with a certain amount of practice, you should begin to hold your images longer and longer.

This can be a very frustrating technique, so make sure you do not get flustered; because if you do you will only be defeating yourself.

Find Yourself

Lie flat on your back and perform one of the pre-flight routines you feel comfortable with. Ask yourself, "Where is my consciousness located in this body?" You are a pinpoint of consciousness. Where are you located? Are you deep within your chest? Are you in the center of your brain near what is called the pineal gland? I picture myself about two or three inches behind my eyes. Look there!

As you search for yourself, casually relinquish control of your arms and legs, as if they were no longer a part of you. Tell yourself you no longer have the desire to feel them. Repeat this step for the upper and lower torso.

This will narrow down the area you have left to look for your consciousness. At this point you may feel a vibration or shaking. You may feel yourself falling backwards through the mattress. Don't fight it! You may also feel as if you are having breathing problems. If you didn't have breathing problems before you started, this may be a sign of the paralysis. You might be at the point of disconnection from the physical. The previous sensations have been some of my largest hurdles. Mainly because the feelings are a little unpleasant (to say the least!) and generally triggered a fight or flee instinct, more often flee. So don't panic! Those of you who reach this disconnection point will soon get used to it. If nothing has happened, yet you feel disconnected, you may need to focus on floating upward. Just repeat two or three times, "I want to float upward."

★ RETROSPECTIVE FINAL

Many things have happened that are not included in this book. As I stated earlier, I have had the paralysis from the age of four. To date that equates to approximately 35 years. I have had numerous "waking up in my dream's" or lucid dream experiences prior to finding out they were really OBEs. Only in the last two or three years have I become aware of the multi-dimensional possibilities of a consciously controlled OBE.

The subject matter in this book primarily addresses the last two years. I believe that I am about to make many unimaginable discoveries. The more I have learned, the more confidence I have been able to build. The more confidence I build, the further I've traveled.

I have been told there are no time restrictions on or above the astral plane. Past and future are alleged to be accessible to the soul traveler. This alone may suggest infinite possibilities.

GLOSSARY OF TERMS

All That Is—the highest consciousness of all; the Light; the Source; the creator; God.

Astral Body—or star body, the word astral literally means relating to the stars; a containment vehicle for the soul/consciousness whose very fabric is comprised of astral substance.

Astral Plane—one of the many levels of consciousness that the mind/soul can perceive. See Planes of Consciousness.

Astral Travel/Projection—to separate or eject astral matter away from the physical body, this matter can then be used to contain the consciousness.

Abort Sequence—this term is used to describe the barely audible moaning which is a signal to be shaken or awakened in order to reconnect with the physical body.

Dogma—a doctrine or belief that is considered fixed and unchangeable.

Enigma—a puzzle; an occurrence that is obscure and difficult to understand.

Higher Self—The God consciousness in all humans; a type of super consciousness; the soul/mind.

Interrupted Sleep Technique (IST)—this is the phrase used to describe a particular sleeping pattern where a person wakes up in the middle of the night, gets up for a couple of hours then goes back to bed. Used to increase the chances of achieving soul travel.

Mahanta—light giver; one who has achieved the highest state of consciousness, a state of God consciousness; the spiritual leader of Eckankar.

Metaphysical—a philosophy focused on the study of the ultimate causes and foundational nature of things.

NDE—Near Death Experience; usually occurs after an extreme trauma to the body, but sometimes occurs when there is only a danger of loss of life.

OBE—Out of Body Experience; a term used to describe the consciousness being displaced or projected from the physical body.

Oversoul—an entity or being that has progressed far beyond the limitations of reality as we understand it; a co-worker with God.

Paralysis State—also known as night paralysis; the lack of physical mobility after achieving a state of altered consciousness.

Glossary of Terms

Personality Self—a part of the psyche that manages our day-to-day lives; a part of us highly influenced by the ego.

Planes of Consciousness—according to esoteric teachings there are multiple levels of awareness and or consciousness. These lower levels have been labeled the physical, astral, causal, mental and etheric.

Repeater—a term that is affectionately used to describe the type of soul that is slow or resistant to evolve; a soul that quickly reincarnates without adequate planning; a type "D" soul on the spiritual arc chart.

Soul Travel—used to describe events similar to OBE and astral projection; a term primarily used by the Eckankar Society.

The Light—a term used in books such as *Embraced by the Light* by B. Eadie, *Saved by the Light* by D. Brinkley; the Light has been described by near death experiencers as an angel, Jesus, and sometimes even God.

Third Eye—a sometimes dormant ability to see multi-dimensional realities or substances; an invisible portal or view port located between ones physical eyes.

Training Wheels—a catch-all phrase to categorize the techniques and beliefs that are no longer used or required.

Vibration—used to describe a rapid oscillation or shaking which appears to be physical but is not; tremors which are usually felt during altered states of consciousness, generally after a significant period of meditation.

White Light—a tool used to protect oneself from negative encounters with one or more non-physical beings; a type of visualization; a spiritual shield created by the imagination.

Reference Books

Seth Speaks — Jane Roberts

Life Between Life — Joel Whitton

Saved By the Light — Dannion Brinkley

Journeys Out of the Body —Robert Monroe

Far Journeys — Robert Monroe

Search for the Truth — Ruth Montegomery

The Education of Oversoul #7 — Jane Roberts

The Seth Material — Jane Roberts

Encyclopedia of Ancient and Forbidden Knowledge — Zolar

The Magic Power Of Witchcraft — Gavin and Frost

Out On A Limb — Shirley MacLaine

The Art of Loving — Eric Fromm

Real Magic— Wayne Dyer

A Course In Miracles — Foundation For Inner Peace

If you would like to order more copies of Soul Traveler or wish to share your own out-of-body experience, please write to :

Verity Press Publishing

P.O. Box 31

Covina, CA 91723

Or you may contact the author through America On Line—SOLTRAVLER @ AOL.COM